WHEN GOD SAYS GO

Velma Trayham

Preface

I DECIDED TO WRITE this book as a testament to the mighty power of God. I would not be here on earth right now, if it was not for God's divine intervention upon my life. I'm sharing my story as a source of inspiration and encouragement. If God can change me and my life around, I assure you that he can do the same for you. No situation is too big for God to handle. It doesn't matter how your life start, it does matter how you end. All you need is God's touch upon your life! You will either wake up and begin to live your best life or you can continue to live an average mediocre life, the choice is yours.

I survived a troubled childhood, I survived hurt and betrayal, I survived failing several times and most recent I survived a car accident that should have left me dead. From one obstacle to another, and reality finally kicked in, God was trying to get my attention! God was trying to refine me, transform my mind and the way that I thought, he was trying to place me where I needed to go. I resisted my "Go" moments many times in life. I did things on my own, I moved forward when I was supposed to be staying still. I stood still when I should've been going. I didn't understand God's timing, and as a result I had a wakeup call.

My prayer is that you find my story, the good, the bad, and the truth very helpful. I've been high and low in business and in my life. When I learned to surrender and follow Gods path, allowing the Holy Spirit to guide me is when the best things in my life truly started to amplify. My businesses are thriving, money is chasing me down, God sent me the love of my life and everything is going according to Gods plan for my life. Here is what you should know, it did not come easy, I had to work for it!

I've written some special prayers that were given to me by the Holy Spirit that are included at the end of this book. These prayers have been composed to help you start your journey. I encourage you to pray endlessly while reading this book, especially between chapters, and seek out your faith, your purpose, and to really listen for the voice of God.

It doesn't stop here, after you read the book I would love to stay connected with you, there will be many more series where I feature women across that world that have embraced their Go moments. I want to hear from you, I want to help you grow; I want to help you become the best version of you. My mission is to Educate & Inspire women from all over the world and from all walks of life find spiritual healing through Christ and teach them business education (the things they don't teach us in school) the real keys to success and living a life of abundance while also educating on how to become financially free. The best way to get to the top is to learn from those who are already there. I am learning more and more that so many people are in a rat race by default because they simply don't know what to do.

It's not what we don't know that hurt us, it's what we don't know that we don't know. All successful people have mentors and coaches, I've made millions of dollars and one of my strategies is aligning myself with people who have been able to teach me what I don't know. My mission is to help over a million women all over the world do better, be better, break barriers and live the life that God has promised us all, if we simply follow his path for our lives.

Visit my website for more information and you can also join my mailing list to stay on top of all the upcoming business and faith summits, private retreats and much more. We are in this together.

www.velmatrayham.com

With abundant blessings headed your way,

Velma   Trayham

Acknowledgements

THE LOVE OF MY life, Christopher Barber, for being there for me, loving me, supporting me and believing in me.

My strong sisters in Christ that shared their moments in the book Gwennetta Wright, Nicole Stoll and Nikole Mccoy.

Helene Vece for her creativity and for helping me to arrange my thoughts and words, bringing my vision into reality.

Pastor Tony Ervin for being obedient to God's calling and praying on and over my life- not just for the accident, but for really being a prayer warrior and spiritual authority.

Alan A. Powell, my mentor. He has taught me to be a strong business woman and has been the true meaning of a support system.

My Boys; Mauni Harris, Chrisarno Delaney and Chrisopher Jayden Barber

My mom, Elizabeth Trayham, and my entire Trayham Family- Jamorcus, Tyeshia, Miracle, Latricia, Tacora, Brenda Smith .. xoxoxoxo

My spiritual mothers: Genet Chenier and Karen Carter Richards,

And to everyone who has supported me along my journey. I love you all! You are always in my heart and spirit. I am forever grateful for your support!

FOREWORD BY:

Apostle Tony Ervin

I'll never forget the month I spent preparing to go to Amsterdam for a weeklong conference after returning from Haiti and preaching at a leadership conference with my Apostle. The Lord had been dealing with me in a strong manner regarding the body of Christ and the chosen vessels of His Kingdom. As I was in consecration and mediation, spending time with the Holy Spirit on March 10, 2016, and preparing for the conference in Amsterdam; the Holy Spirit spoke very clear to me instructing me to call Velma Trayham quickly and pray with her.

Velma and I had established a relationship a few months prior to March 10th. She was invited to our Houston location by one of the members. Our congregation and Church had recently launched in the Houston area and Ms. Trayham assisted in the development of our branding with a new logo and website. She was working with us to help establish the visibility of our new branch. However, we both sensed the Lord had established this friendship for a greater purpose and reason. Through her constant visitation of the ministry, I began to realize that Velma Trayham desired to be closer to the Lord and to know His will and plan for her life. I began to pray earnestly for her ability to know God in a deeper and intimate way.

On March 10, 2016, the Holy Spirit instructed me to call and pray for Velma. Immediately, I stopped what I was doing to reach out to her. When Velma answered the phone, I asked her was she available for prayer. She stated she was driving somewhere, but she would "pull over to receive prayer". I sensed that God was interrupting both our schedules by calling us into prayer at such an unusual time of the day. I was in Orlando, Florida at the time, and Velma had just moved to Atlanta, Ga. As I began to pray for Velma over the phone, prophetic utterance came up concerning her present situation and God's future for her life! Divine impartations were released upon Velma for strength and protection for the journey ahead.

We closed the prayer; not knowing the very next day was the reason God instructed us to pray. The prayer God directed me to pray for Velma on March 10th protected her from a horrible car wreck the very next day!

I honestly believe that if Velma Trayham insisted that her schedule was too full to pray just then, she would not be here to write this powerful book and share her testimony. I truly thank God for Velma's obedience to the voice of God. Her obedience to the Lord has truly changed her life. I want to thank God, and Velma Trayham, for giving me this wonderful opportunity to be a part of what God is doing in her life and within my ministry.

I pray this book touches your life in a unique way. May God's presence go before you as you conquer the land of promise! Deuteronomy 31:8.

Apostle Tony Ervin

A Tree of Life Fellowship

Tree-oflifechurch.org

MEET THE AUTHOR OF WHEN GOD SAYS GO- VELMA TRAYHAM

Christian Marketing Expert, Real Estate Investor, Author And The Award-winning Founder Of ThinkZILLA PR & Consulting Group, LLC.

VELMA TRAYHAM GREW UP in Houston, Texas third ward and spite of her troubled childhood; she was determined to rise above the many obstacles and challenges she faced. Velma gained vast experience building her own companies while also helping others to do the same. Velma discovered her passion for inspiring and educating others at the early stages of her career. Velma's Mindset that *temporary failure doesn't mean permanent defeat* has been her consistent message throughout her professional career.

Leveraging her marketing background as a platform, Velma launched THINKZILLA PR & Consulting Group. She has worked with industry leaders, such as; Bishop Jakes, Daymond John, Meagan Good, Houston's Mayor- Sylvester Turner, and other prominent leaders as her company, and her expertise, grew. Velma's own business mentors include serial entrepreneur Alan "AP" Powell and self-help books by Zig Ziglar,

Trayham is the force behind—and the CEO of—the THINKZILLA PR & Consulting Group. Her workshops, mentoring programs, and marketing systems have helped companies see 200 percent growth in just one year. Some of Velma's many accomplishments include receiving multiple proclamations by the City of Houston Mayor, as well as being featured in publications such as; Defender Magazine, Sister 2 Sister, Rolling Out, Houston Forward Times, Houston Press, Black News, Dallas Weekly, African American News, Jet, and Texas Oil & Gas.

Velma is a frequent speaker at industry events from Atlanta to Houston and across the southern region. As a keynote speaker, Velma encourages audiences to live their dreams and not let failure become a state of mind while also touching on life changing business education tips.

Velma has written several other business books to include: "AFTER THE PIVOT; REAL ADVICE ON HOW TO SURVIVE A BUSINESS PIVOT AND MAKE MONEY." Velma continues her journey by leaning on God to provide a clear and practical blueprint for personal success, drawn directly from her own life experiences.

Among the prestigious awards and honors bestowed upon Velma, she is immensely proud to be the recipient of the Top Entrepreneur Award by Houston Power Professionals, Faces of Black Houston by Defender Honoree, Stellar Leadership Award by Lighthouse Church, Honored by Who's Who Worldwide Branding Executives, Top PR Firm by Houston Top Music Award Show, Top Business Leader for Secret Society Media Awards, and Fabric of a Women Humanitarian Award.

$Contents$

FLASHY ME,
A PUBLIC "WRECK"

Lessons Learned, Promoting Your Own Victory

HOW DO YOU DEFINE success? Is it with money? Power? Material things? Public Perception? Maybe it is simply based on where you started as a kid and where you are now. A few years ago, I would have defined success as material things, Flashy cars, designer clothes,

Multiple companies… the list went on and on. There was something missing from my list, which was God. I attributed all my success to luck, hard work, and a lot of me.

Yes, I thought I had it really going on, in fact you couldn't tell me nothing. I was an unstoppable, woman who was leading in my profession of Marketing and Public Relations, or so I thought. Then suddenly the Holy Spirit told me to GO, leave my hometown and start a new life in a whole different state. Not only was

I led to GO but when I left I had a life changing wreck, I was hit by a semi-truck with no seatbelt on and not to mention not one airbag deployed in a brand-new car. I was driving, on the phone, eating, and I was headed to a business meeting that I had no business going to, and further into the story you'll learn why I should not have been going to a meeting.

My Lexus was totaled, the entire front end of my car was on the ground, and glass from my windshield was everywhere. My life flashed in front of me! This was the moment that I realized that God had a purpose for my life, and I had to learn that my purpose did *not* start with focusing on my own self-centered desires. Everything I had done up to that moment was no more than a lesson from God, and it was God's hand that helped me walk away from that horrible accident without even a scratch. This was my 'Go moment'.

We must understand that positions of power in life come with great responsibility. We must prove our ability to not only run these positions, but do so from a place of Godly growth. I would not be honest with you if I told you that I was not God's finest creature walking the planet a few years ago; I had all the appearances of success, but I was very empty on the inside. There was a void there, I could not understand what I was missing, but I *was* missing something and it was something that money could not buy.

The reason I can tell you this is because I made my first million in my early twenties, and I'm not saying this to impress anyone, I'm simply making a point here that no matter how much money you have, money don't buy happiness. Looking back at myself, I was spiritually blind, spiritually dead, and lost. The journey has been rough, because there was a time I lost it all many times and had to start all over again, simply because I was doing things my way and not Gods way.

I always knew that God created me for something much bigger. Thanks to my business failures that I learned early on in life when I failed many times, I never gave up. I just kept on going until I finally learned how to turn my failures into success. I thank God now for all my past failures, I realize now that they were all part of my journey. Most people knew there was something more than a beautiful smile happening with me. The accident that changed my life was my rebirth, my new life, a fresh start, a way for God to really lead and guide me, giving me a life of peace, happiness, and joy. A life full of blessings, freedom, and abundance.

The other women in this book didn't experience a wreck, but they did have powerful 'Go moments' of their own; words of the Spirit of God reaching into their soul and changing their lives in a moment.

When God Says Go is the ultimate blueprint to help you overcome obstacles and stumbling blocks that have kept you from reaching your fullest potential. Your Destiny is waiting for you! Let go of everything and trust God. Are you ready to listen to the voice of God when he tells you to Go? I encourage you to embrace this journey; we aren't *truly* living until we've found our true purpose in life.

FINDING SPIRITUAL WEALTH

THERE ARE WAYS GOD hints for us to really listen to what he wants to get through to us. Even in the Bible, the story of Ester refers to the power of purpose and where God wants you planted without ever mentioning "God". As a marketing consultant and public relations professional, I always say, go where the data leads. Well, I'm here to let you know that your gut is the basis for your data and you must go where God leads.

Many people say God's timing is the right timing, but are we always willing to watch for the signs? Before I packed up my successful business in Houston to move to Atlanta, I was doing well. There was no reason in the world for me to leave my comfort and success zone. But I was sick and tired of living life with no purpose. I was tired of just living for me and I knew that God had something of much greater purpose for me to accomplish not for me but for him.

I wasn't a bad person. I did make some bad decisions, as we all do. Making bad decisions is part of the journey; God uses our trials and bad mistakes to shape us into the beautiful people we were created to be. This is why we need God. We often forget that God created us, how can we expect to live and prosper without the owner and the manual? It's like buying a Mercedes, if the brakes go out, an inexperienced mechanic attempting to fix the brakes with no manual is going to screw up big time and make a bigger mess; the experienced mechanic knows he needs the manual that came with the vehicle.

I was on my knees praying, seeking God's direction and purpose for my life; the spirit of God spoke to me and told me to leave Houston. I was confused; that other little voice in the back of my mind was asking, 'leave for what? Why would I leave?' It sounded stupid at the time, in fact, many people questioned why the voice of God telling me to do such a thing. My youngest baby had just started pre-k and my business was going well. But God told me to go. You will always know its God when the instructions are opposite of what your flesh wants you to do. That very day I left without knowing where I was going, what I was going to do, or how I was going to do anything. This was the true epitome of Steve Harvey's book "Jump".

It is important to not pray for what you want and need, but to pray for what God wants you to do. God wants to use each one of us, but often we are afraid to be used by God. In fact, we allow ourselves to be used by everyone, except God. Our boss, friends, family, wives, and husbands use us, so why are we afraid to surrender and be used by God? What do you pray for? Do you pray for wisdom, knowledge, and discernment? Those are the things we should be praying for, but most people are always asking God for things, is this something you do? Admittedly, I did. And this is where spiritual maturity and growth becomes crucial to the journey of your success.

Here is how this book will change your life; I have provided some great Bible scriptures and other religious resources to back-up my story of faith. Further, I offer life-changing advice for both personal and professional development, which I've learned through my own life experiences. The religious stories are not meant to bore you, but to help you understand the Who, What, Where, and Why behind what God promises in the Bible! I strongly suggest you study these short Biblical stories, references, and quotes; they will help discover your untapped greatness and your sure path to success and *really* living; not just surviving but really THRIVING.

Let's get started by pondering a few stories from the Bible that are prime examples of how God's work and hand in our lives can really make a difference in your growth; start by reading the book of Hebrews 11:8-12. If you don't have your Bible, here is the basic text:

"By faith Abraham obeyed when he was called to go out to a place that he was to receive as an inheritance. And he went out, not knowing where he was going. By faith he went to live in the land of promise, as in a foreign land, living in tents with Isaac and Jacob, heirs with him of the same promise. For he was looking forward to the city that has foundations, whose designer and builder is God."

Faith is the substance of things not seen and the evidence of things hoped for. Most of us claim we trust God, but our actions really don't align with our words. There are three very important elements to faith; hoping, waiting patiently, and trusting. My biggest mistake in the past was mouthing the words "I trust God", but I was anxiously forcing things to happen how I wanted them to happen. And because of that, I delayed my own success and God given destiny for a long time. In business, we tend to rely on our own self-will, but guess what? We were wrong and we would never get ahead that way.

You can't have faith and worry at the same time! Your own desires will always want to improve on the current moment or situation. For me, it was always striving to be perfect. Perfection does not exist, but I wanted to be seen as perfect. That really crippled me. I had to learn to love myself and use my weaknesses as a stepping stone, imperfections and all. There is only one perfect person and that's Jesus, our lord and savior.

If you stop and stand still, let go of the self-will, and stand in faith God will lead you along the right direction. He will give you the desires of your heart, if you would just trust him and fully commit yourself to him. Most people try to pick and choose which parts of their lives they want to give God; it doesn't work that way. We must totally surrender, ask for forgiveness, and allow God to make us new in mind, body, and spirit.

I always tell people the only way to fully surrender is to really want to change, stop complaining, take responsibility for your own actions, accept who you are, and ask God to do the rest. And trust me God is near to everyone who calls and invites him. Don't be afraid to let him in. Stop whining about your problems, stop thinking negatively, and stop thinking you know everything or that you are owed something. If you can begin to reprogram your mind, you will allow the peace of God to take over. Most importantly, you will teach yourself how to stand still in faith, which is vital in any business and in your personal life.

Going back to the story of Abraham, think about how he had to be a strong believer in the feeling of "Go" that was put in his heart, otherwise would he really risk everything he had? He walked blindly into a situation that was dark and didn't offer a safety net.

Look at your own life. Are you afraid to go? Your Go moment may be a toxic relationship, a job that you have evolved out of, friends that you need to let go, a city you need to depart from. If you miss your Go moment, you may miss your shot at your best life. Think about it this way - when you have everything to gain, you can stand to lose a few things. In fact, sometimes you *must* lose to win. Whatever it is you do have; would you be willing to walk away from it because God promised you a better life? Do you *really* trust God?

What I like about Abraham's story is his example to live by faith. To put down all that we know, and everything we think we want or have worked so hard for, to "Go" where the Holy Spirit is leading us. You must learn to walk by faith and not by sight. When you pray, you should not expect God to answer your prayers immediately without carrying your own cross and giving up your sinful desires for him.

Most people only pray when things are going badly, what sense does that make? You can't use Jesus like that. You are to pray always, when things are good, great, bad, and indifferent. God knows your motives and intentions, thus if you're praying and nothing is happening, check your motives!

To be successful in life you must do the right thing. My success principles are simple; honesty, loyalty, patience, love, and prayer; there is no way around these principles. You will not always reap the benefits immediately; just like when a woman is pregnant, it's painful and feels like it takes forever, but after she delivers, there is so much joy. In the same way, doing right in a world where most people are doing wrong may not feel good at the time. Are you ready to die in order to live? I can tell you, from my own journey, that I was not always ready.

Another Bible passage that I want to share with you, before you start your journey to success -and so you understand why it is important to "Go" when you get the calling- is Acts 7:54-60. This part of the Bible reflects upon the Holy Spirit and the rewards and benefits of being an ambassador for God.

"Now when they heard these things they were enraged, and they ground their teeth at him. But he, full of the Holy Spirit, gazed into heaven and saw the glory of God, and Jesus standing at the right hand of

God. And he said, "Behold, I see the heavens opened, and the Son of Man standing at the right hand of God." But they cried out with a loud voice and stopped their ears and rushed together at him. Then they cast him out of the city and stoned him. And the witnesses laid down their garments at the feet of a young man named Saul. And as they were stoning Stephen, he called out, "Lord Jesus, receive my spirit." And falling to his knees he cried out with a loud voice, "Lord, do not hold this sin against them." And when he had said this, he fell asleep."

We all must make hard decisions in life. Your decisions *will* impact the lives of other people. You will become discouraged. Just after my accident, I didn't immediately jump for joy that God allowed me to walk away. I was terrified. I was untrusting. I was angry. I had to remind myself that God's plan for my life was much bigger than what my mind could create.

The passages and verses of the Bible I have shared with you in this chapter are important moments for you to sit back and ponder your feelings, your approach to God, and how you want to respond when the Spirit calls you to move forward in life. This isn't something that you should breeze through. It is very important that you meditate on, and trust, my warnings about fear, hesitation, and temptation.

In early 2016, when the spirit of God led me to leave my hometown of Houston, Texas, I was leaving it *all* behind. Fed up with everything, I was mentally exhausted and tired of myself. I was hungry for change.

I remembered all I did was pray and fast. I would pray four to five times a day, I was intentional. I *needed* divine intervention. I needed God himself to come down on earth and touch me. I was praying for guidance, wisdom, and understanding. I asked God to open my heart and teach me to do things by his way and not my own. I was reading the Bible, I began meditating to understand what God wanted to do in my life and even in the lives of others around me. That's the hard part because there is usually two voices we hear and how do we know which is the voice of God? That's the tricky part and that means we must really be in tune.

"Ask, and it shall be given to you; seek, and you shall find; knock, and it shall be opened to you. For everyone who asks receives, and he who seeks finds, and to him who knocks it shall be opened. (NAS, Matthew 7:7-11). God will answer our prayers and give us everything we need and more. But a wise parent will not give a child everything he or she wants. Similarly, prayer is not a magical trick to get anything we want or a "quick fix" for problems that we should solve ourselves. God answers prayer requests in His own way and in His own time, and will not grant requests that are against His holy and wise purposes, are selfish in nature, are not in our best long-term interest, or those made with impure motives.

I wanted to do the right thing. I wanted to overcome all of my past hurt and everything I dealt with as a child. My mom was a drug addict. I didn't receive a lot of love and affection as a child. Growing up was pretty rough for me because I felt that people were out to hurt me. It wasn't until recently I realized how being so guarded was keeping me stuck. If you need to, write the following down. Trust me, it is important you place this passage from ExporeFaith.org somewhere within your daily view:

"The power of prayer is the power that comes to us when we realize that God can be our point of reference in the midst of all the confusions of our daily lives, the steadfastness of God rather than the incomplete, fragile inconstancies of ourselves. It's the power that comes when we're able to be centered, anchored in a belief and rooted in a Truth, which is stronger and deeper than the day-to-day truths we struggle with.

The power of prayer is the constant renewal of perspective. Prayer opens our eyes. It extends our horizons. It sheds light into the darkness of our fears and our sorrows, our hopes and joys, our shame and our pride. It gives us innovative ways of seeing life and relationships, of understanding work and the cost of growing.

The power of prayer is real and palpable. You can feel it and know it and depend on it. It comes to us as a gift, but we need to do our part as well. God calls us to pray and through our prayer, God empowers us and gives us strength."

Don't pray out of routine. When I decided to make my change, I shut myself down. Everything was put on hold and set aside so I could focus on God. After all, I wanted God to focus on me. I wanted His help so I had to be not only willing to listen, but ready to too. I couldn't be distracted and I couldn't be detoured.

Tears started to stream down my face. I didn't really understand why, during this time in my life I would cry so hard and so much. I felt like I didn't really have anyone I could talk to. I felt like my spirit was in prison. I was admitting self-defeat. I couldn't do life on my own. This is hard for anyone to do. But I did it. I admitted the need for help. I admitted to my shortcomings, my failures. To get help, we must first admit we have a problem. I was thankful I finally learned I had a problem. For a long time, I thought I was perfectly fine

When I started to pray, I realized that fear is a strange and useless emotion - yet most of us are guided by it. The more I prayed, the more I started to understand that I was living my life out of fear to run from feelings of fear that had kept me in bondage. Fear of failure, fear of rejection, fear that we're just not enough — fear is a common current that runs through all of our lives. And if we let it, fear can keep us locked up in the prison of the comfortable and predictable.

There is a way fear can serve a valuable purpose, helping us break through the frustration to achieve the life we truly desire. That's right — if you allow it to, fear can become your ultimate motivator. In your mind, if you have no choice but to succeed — if achieving your goal is an absolute must — then nothing else matters. Sacrifices won't even be a question. Excuses go out the window. You'll do whatever it takes to make it happen. Period.

As I prayed, and I addressed my fear, I had an "aha" moment, as Oprah Winfrey might say. The Holy Spirit spoke to me. The fear I was feeling and hiding for years - it no longer mattered. I was inspired and empowered. I prayed with intent, I kept an open heart and open ear, and I was not only ready for a change but also *willing* to change. God had said, "Go" and I had my mission.

The Holy Spirit had inspired me to leave everything behind and to start over. This meant leave everything behind. What I did next was the equivalent to dipping a toe in the pond of listening to God. In fact, many people call it selective hearing. I heard "Go" and I had it in my heart to follow, but I wasn't ready to leave everything behind, so God made sure he would show me not only that he was there for me - but that leaving everything behind in his answer truly meant leaving everything behind!

I started to prepare to leave. I headed to my mother's home to get my son's shot records and then to hit the road.   As soon as I told my mom I was leaving she looked at me with the most puzzled explanation. She wasn't ready for it and she wasn't happy that I was taking her grandbaby out of state without more than a quick goodbye.

My son and I headed for the road and we were moving ourselves, literally, forward. I was debating between Nashville and Atlanta as I sang along to the gospel music on the radio. The Lexus was the last piece of me, as far as material things were concerned. Everything else I let go, sold it, or left it standing.

The music filled the car and worry filled my son's eyes. When you think about the move that I was making, it was really a bold act of faith. I was out in the world with a crazy dream and a movement in my heart and I had no solid evidence, or even predictable proof, that anything was going to work out for me. I was stepping out in faith knowing that re-rooting my son could cause him a social setback. I trusted God anyway.

My son and I finally arrived in Atlanta, where the Holy Spirit told me to go. It was a drive based on faith and an ardent desire for change. My family, friends, and even some of my clients thought I had lost my mind. As a strategic businesswoman, most of my moves are cool and calculated, but this one was certainly not.

Almost a month into living in Atlanta, I enrolled my son in Tayo Reed Performing Arts, a private school in Atlanta, Ga. The day before my son was supposed to be in school, the Holy Spirit was trying to tell me that it wasn't time for me to do business. I was ordered not to seek out new clients or to give in to the itch to sell my company's services. Old habits are hard to break. For many business professionals, time truly is money. If you're wasting time, you're losing money.

I'll never forget the day before my accident. I received a call from Prophet Tony Ervin from A Tree of Life Fellowship (whom also I am grateful to have as a foreword writer for this book). My company had assisted him with his church website and rebranding a few months earlier. His exact words to me were, "Woman of God I need to pray with you immediately, The Spirit of God showed me where the enemy is trying to take you out." I stopped everything I was doing; I pulled my car over and allowed the Prophet to pray for me.

He started praying in the spirit in tongues and there was true and real power in his voice. I was somewhat concerned, but not enough to detour the plan I had for the next day, which was to attend a meeting that I had no business taking until I was released from God to resume with business. As I was praying for things to happen on my time, I was tempted with a potential client meeting the following day. I wasn't supposed to be focused on business at all, but the flesh in me was.

I should have been trusting God! One thing I've learned is we can't worry *and* trust God at the same time. It's one or the other. As Prophet Tony Ervin's oddly timed phone call was meant to warn and help validate what the Holy Spirit was trying to tell me, I took the call along with the prayer and preceded with my day as though God didn't send his messenger to save my life.

On the next day after dropping my son off to school, I started to feel very happy because my son was happy and excited to start his new school, it didn't seem that all the sudden changes were causing him any issues as far as his emotional or social health was concerned. I was grateful that he seemed 'OK' and was not having any immediate adjustment issues.

I got into my car, adjusted my makeup and then my mirrors, and hit the freeway headed downtown Atlanta for my meeting. I had my music going and then I got a call from a friend on Facetime. I was driving, and eating at the same time. I know; I was putting others in danger. I could have killed someone, never mind me, but that was typical me - always thinking about myself!

I was told by God not to work for 6 weeks. I didn't trust God. I didn't want to listen to what the Holy Spirit was saying when it came to not working. Like Adam and Eve in the garden, I was given orders and I disobeyed. I decided that I could solve my own problems, not God, and left Him out of the equation.

I ran a red light at a major intersection in Atlanta. A semi-truck hit me and then I was hit again by another car. The Lexus spun around like a spinning top toy. Not a single airbag deployed, as they should have. I saw glass everywhere, and I heard people screaming "is she alive?"

We were all in disbelief. Not only was I alive, despite being hit by the semi-truck, but I was able to walk away without a single broken bone, in spite of the fact that my airbags didn't deployed. I had a bruised leg, but that was it. I took the trip to the hospital to check if there was internal bleeding anywhere, which there was not.

I had walked away from what very easily could have been a fatal accident. Everything about the accident pointed to the fact that it *should* have been the end of my life. God cleaned my slate for me; He sent me a message. I was allowed to live and carry on, but I had to do so obediently going forward. Life Flight rushed me to the hospital, they could not believe I was still alive. God's angels were all around me; I was covered by the blood of Jesus Christ. The crash that should have ended by life was the very thing that helped me really start to live!

The Bible is filled with stories of miracles. I am a walking testimony of God's love and his ability to grant second, third, even hundredth chances in life. His mercy, His protection, and His desire to bless us, so we can help others while here, is awe-inspiring. When I was released from the hospital, again only as a precautionary partial admin, I watched the videotape from the street camera of my accident and wondered *how did I survive this?* God has a way of showing us his power and work in our lives, and often it's done in a way that we can't take any credit for.

A ROADMAP FOR SUCCESS

———✦———

W HEN YOUR "GO" MOMENT hits, or at least as it is tempting and hinting at you, the question you will have to deal with is the self-doubt that will arise in your mind. Self-doubt hinders change. You can't change, or really explore and embrace your "Go" moment when you are dealing with self-doubt, fear, or toxic relationships - and I know a thing or two about toxic relationships.

First, when your inner doubts bubble up, be quick to respond and remember that these thoughts are straight from a place of negativity, if not the Evil one himself. Don't let the feelings of self-doubt or negativity spin out of control or grow from a whisper to a stream of discouraging sentences. Instead, talk back to that doubtful part of yourself. You must use these moments to praise God and to remember that you are blessed in your life, regardless of the circumstances.

For me, I acknowledge the negative thoughts and I pray on them. I spend time to make sure I disrupt the thought pattern and bad feelings associated with self-doubt and I make it a point to stop that inner self-doubter from taking over my life, my decisions, and from doubting God's word or his hints and nudges that could lead to a "Go" moment.

You also can't be fake with who you are. There is no faking it until you make it. That's a lie that is a trendy way to skip corners in life and make yourself feel like you are gaining traction either in your personal or professional life. You must be real with God and yourself.

The action wasn't easy. No, I had to forge ahead. I had to understand and then trust that God wasn't going to let me fail or fall, but that I had to move myself forward and trust Him. Failure is never an option. If you don't succeed, you've learned a lesson, and therefore you've gained something. When you fail you are simply gaining knowledge, so if something doesn't work out - there was a lesson in it as a tool for you to grow. I use this thought process often in my personal life and in business. Remember, self- doubt wants you to shy away from the "Go" moments and be fearful of failure. If you remove failure as an option, the need to reason with self-doubt goes away, too.

Self-doubts are most often spiritual monsters in your head. They are sent to distract and detour you from your success and your "Go" moments. This is the devil's way, to use your mind against you, to keep you from making changes, and to keep you within the comfort zone. Maybe, to even keep you addicted, in a toxic relationship, feeding sin, or oppressed from God. If you look to the past and see how well things have gone many times despite those self-doubts, I promise you that it will become easier to let go of the self-doubt and to focus on the more likely positive outcome and to act when the urge to "Go" comes around.

We live in a self-obsessed "I" culture. When we focus on what other people think about us, or what we think other people are thinking about us, we are not focusing on God or what He wants for us. I can't tell you how much white noise there is with social media, regular media, and people's own problems and worries that blanket their ability, sadly, to care enough about whatever inner self-doubt that you may be focused on.

For example, you may be focused on how big your nose is. You think about this a million times a day. And you probably think other people are always thinking about your nose, too. This is negative self-talk, and it leads to negative self-esteem. These feelings, these worries, this self-doubt and obsession about what others may be thinking about you are not ways to fulfill your destiny- they are thoughts that take you away from your "Go" moment and are in direct disobedience to God.

You can't be successful and worry at the same time. You can't trust God and worry at the same time. And trust me, what you worry about and what others may think or say are usually on two entirely different levels of severity. Be still and remind yourself that the truth is that people don't really care that much about what you do or not do. They are consumed by white noise and their own challenges. You have to live for God and follow God's path, not the path of what you think other people want or expect you to do.

Self-doubt also gets us in trouble with our relationships. You need to be in a supportive and God filled relationship or you will encounter self-doubt and this can lead to attracting the wrong type of energy and the worst types of people. This means a clean and clear mind to focus on being positive, removing self-doubt, and refraining from negative behaviors so you can identify your "Go" moment. The sex, the drugs, and the crazy music may be fogging up your windshield, leaving you unable to see the road ahead.

Toxic relationships may appear to be happy relationships, so you must consider the foundation. Is it all about how good the sex is? Is it all about how the two of you appear to the outside world? Is it all about the money or what you can gain? Or what you can provide to be able to keep that person at your side? Is it all about public perception? Is it all just being with someone just because you don't want to be alone or just because you have a child together? Do you feel like you have sacrificed yourself so you can say you have a significant other?

Relationships should always focus to put God first, without any substances or ulterior motives. You shouldn't have to pay for a person's love. The materialistic side of things is okay, if the love and movement is *real*. Money cannot buy happiness and if you find yourself in this type of relationship, you had better get out of it before it's too late, because if you lost it all, that person may not be there for you because it simply wasn't real from the beginning. I've been in relationships where I was given everything I wanted except time, peace, and real love. I've learned that just because someone buys me lots of stuff does not constitute a strong sign of real love. I am priceless and no one can buy me. This is the mentality that we all must adapt to.

The best thing you can do is remember that you are a child of God in search of a better life and an even better way of living. Your "Go" moment can't happen if you are too busy allowing yourself to be blinded by stuff. And, deep down inside, you know when things are not right. You know when the gut feeling is there, but often we ignore how we feel because we are enjoying the right now moments. Learn to look at things long term and ask yourself, *how will this affect me in the future? How will this situation help me grow spiritually?* At the end of the day, if you are not growing, you are not GOING anywhere.

If you're in a toxic relationship, leave. There is no negotiating who you are destined to become. Start with making a promise to cut off all contact, change phone numbers, use a feature that I absolutely love: "block", erase all old social media posts that could remind you of the person and prepare yourself to receive the relationship that is God sent. You must start with a new outlook and a renewed mind. You need to treat yourself like the child of God that you are, and see yourself as God sees you. Until you cut off the toxic relationship, you will further be delayed from your "Go" moment.

If you are feeling vulnerable, or having issues with self-doubt, you will likely be at risk to go back into your toxic relationship. When these feelings come, pray; asking God to set your mind on things that are good, true, and fulfilling. It's normal to miss your ex and your old habits, stay mindful, however, that missing times that felt good do not mean that he or she was, or is, good for you.

God has a greater purpose for you and you must remind yourself this, should you forget. If you have trouble remembering your own value and the vision you must listen for, think about what you would say to a family member or close friend who wanted to return to a toxic relationship. Think about if your own child was in the relationship with a toxic person, like you were. How would you respond?

Be bold and expect God's favor by making a change (or a few changes) and creating your own roadmap for success in life. Once you have the new map, finding your "Go" moment will be easy.

To start, understand that insanity is doing the same thing repeatedly while expecting different results. Once you decide to leave toxic people, places, and things behind, you can start creating your own change. If you want something to be different in your life, the change must start with you. Always act as if what you want is already on its way to you and a part of your life already. Praise God for what he is going to put in your path going forward. Thank God for the "Go" moment that he is about to share with you. Remember, what's happening in your life isn't necessarily what you want right now. A belief in lack only creates more lack. Self-doubt only creates worry and fear. Creating change from a present place of appreciation and abundance is much more powerful than anything else in the world.

Your "Go" moment requires a set-up for success. You can't afford to miss out on your destiny because of temptation or a life that is not being well lived.

Paul says (2 Cor. 4:3-4), "And even if our gospel is veiled, it is veiled to those who are perishing, in whose case the god of this world [lit., age] has blinded the minds of the unbelieving so that they might not see the light of the gospel of the glory of Christ, who is the image of God." (See, also, Eph. 2:2, NASB margin.)

WEAPONS FOR WAR

O NLY GOD CAN BREAK the chains of who we were in our past. After all, we must not forget that Jesus died on the cross for our sins so that we can live in complete freedom. God does not judge us and certainly we should care less about other sinners, like you and I, judging us. Like my car accident, sometimes it takes the hand of God to help turn things around - even if the situation is scary at first. I am sure, for the man in the Bible named Legion that had demons run from him after having control for an extended period of time, was scary... reference verse (Luke 8:26-39). When Jesus commanded that they leave, the man didn't know what would happen to him- if he would even survive. The touch of God is miraculous upon our lives.

Business is a scary landscape to work within. You must put God first in every aspect of your life, including how you run and operate your business. Sometimes God will tell you to "Go" and sometimes

God will want you to wait. Listen to the Holy Spirit. Do not attempt to handle things yourself without guidance. You may not like the timing, you may have an itch to micro-manage your own situation; be still and let God work.

I've learned to put on God's armor. It is a challenging thing to do, but we must trust God and his timing. Think about where he was in your life up and until now. There is always a place in time where you can pinpoint a fall- or what should have been a fall. Right there, as soon as you reflect on it, is evidence of God's touch in your life.

Most of us have these moments more than once. For me, it was moving away from my comfort zone; also, the car accident. I had the armor of God on that day, despite everything I was doing wrong. Before I go any further, I want to explain what the armor of God is and how you put it on. The phrase "full armor of God "comes from Ephesians 6:13-17: "Therefore put on the full armor of God, so that when the devil comes, you may be able to stand your ground, and after you have done everything, to stand. Stand firm then, with the belt of truth buckled around your waist, with the breastplate of righteousness in place, and with your feet fitted with the readiness that comes from the gospel of peace. In addition to all this, take up the shield of faith, with which you can extinguish all the flaming arrows of the evil one. Take the helmet of salvation and the sword of the Spirit, which is the word of God."

Now that we know what the full armor is, let's talk about how to put the full armor on. Every believer needs to know how to battle with evil people and evil situations. God gives us detailed instructions on how to put on the armor.

Step 1. The Belt of Truth means two things: our hearts and our minds. Practicing truth and being truthful keeps us secure in Christ and this is the most effective area, the belt of truth holds your armor in place. You must commit yourself daily to walking in the light and the truth, blocking out lies and fake things that pop up in your mind.

Step 2. The Breastplate of Righteousness: The devil is constantly attacking us with lies, accusations, guilt, and reminding us of our past sins. Without the breastplate of righteousness, these thoughts will begin to take root in our mind causing us to lose hope and faith, causing us to want to give up. Never forget who you are in Christ. Never forget that Jesus died on the cross for our sins, come boldly into God's presence resisting the devil immediately and constantly.

Step 3. The Shield of Faith: It is right up the devil alley for us to lose faith. The shield of faith not only defends our entire body, but it helps us to stay hopeful. And this is something that we must do every day through prayer; ask God to teach us to stand firm and trust the process. No matter what happens in life, we are to have faith that God will see us through the challenging times. We will always have trouble, but when you have faith and walk with God, He will lead you to peace.

Step 4. Put on your Sword. My sword is the word of God, in other words, The Bible. The Bible is a tool and a roadmap. There were many wise people and there were many people who have had to overcome the same obstacles we face today, so why not get guidance from them and by following God's commands. We must trust in the truth and have confidence in God's word. We must thirst for it and then everything else will come.

Step 5. Pray! I cannot stress the importance of this. Prayer is so powerful. Pray always and about everything. We must stay alert and persistent in our prayers. Sometimes, it may seem that God is far away and our prayers aren't being answered, it's not an overnight process you must stay at it. Pray morning and night, and small prayers throughout the day. Instead of calling your buddy when you have a problem, call on God. At least He can do something about it. Prayer is the answer to 99% of our problems.

Putting on the armor of God comes with having the faith to give up the control you think you have and birth a new you, one who is willing to be patient and willing to trust God to solve things versus trying to do so on your own.

I call this 'briefing before the battle'. Life can change in the blink of an eye and it doesn't take much to shake us. We are fragile and we have breaking points. Regardless if it is personal or business, there is risk in everything when we don't walk out of the house in the morning saying our prayers and wearing God's armor.

I know, you think this is easier said than done. We are all human, which makes us flawed. What I am stressing to you is that God has given us all the protection we need. Second, He always goes before us, fighting all our battles. Third, He reveals to us the plots of the enemy, and the tactics that will be used against us. Finally, He will never allow the enemy to win; God will overcome the plots and schemes of the world, which is why I stand on his promises.

When I was going through all my challenges, I hated life. I was stressed out. I was broken, and I had to learn how to become unbroken and restored. Most people turn to counselors and other specialists, I chose to allow God to be my counselor. In fact, He's the best counselor because He knows us far better than we know ourselves. I am not saying that you should not get some help, if that's the route you want to take, because there are many great counselors and phycologist out there who can help you with restoration. It was my decision to cultivate a relationship with God and allow God to be my counsel.

I was distracted many times by temptation and the urge to give in to fear and self-pity on my journey of becoming a better person. Especially in Atlanta, where there is always something to do, parties, red carpet/celebrity events, and everything else. It takes a strong will to stay focused and to resist temptation. We can't do it alone; we need God's direction every single day. The temptations and daily challenges are far too big for us to handle alone. One word of advice about self-pity, we must really be on guard because it can, and does, creep up on us all.

I call self-pity a demonic trap because when it happens we are unaware of it happening until it's too late. There are several ways to protect your mind against self-pity; always keep praying and thanking God for what you have; we all have many things to be thankful for. It is impossible to feel sorry for yourself and praise God at the same time. You must make thanking God a daily routine to block your mind from temptations and self-pity.

Never think you can solve your problems on your own, in fact, doing so often makes your problems worse. The Bible tells us in Ephesians 6:12, "For our struggle is not against flesh and blood, but against the rulers, against the authorities, against the powers of this dark world and against the spiritual forces of evil in the heavenly realms." You must put on God's full armor to be able to stand up against the devil's tricks and schemes. You must understand what it means to put the full armor on, I'm going somewhere with this friend, by the time you are done reading this book, you will overcome, you will be victorious, you will have a new found outlook on life.

When God was dealing with me, he showed me how I was being distracted by all types of things that were important. This is a prime example of how crafty the devil is; he knows how to keep us distracted. God also began to show me some of my ungodly ways, such as being self-serving. I would always focus on myself first, everything I did started with me in mind. As I grew closer to God, I started to learn that my purpose did not start with me, and if I really wanted to do God's work, I had to put others before myself. The book that really helped me to figure out my God given purpose was, The Purpose Driven Life by Rick Warren. You should pick it up if you haven't already done so. You will gain so much clarity about what God has created you to do and how you should be of service to others.

God blesses you so that you can, in return, *be* a blessing to other people. Everything that you have right now comes from God, and if you do right with it, he will bless you with even more. Some of you may not be experiencing the more right now, but ask yourself, what are giving to others? Who are you helping to grow? Who are you going out of your way to help? What charity organization are you donating to? Are you praying for others? Are you paying your tithes at church? If you're not doing any of these things, I guarantee this is why you are having problems. Another one of my favorite Bible scriptures is Luke 6:38, "Give, and it will be given to you. A good measure, pressed down, shaken together and running over, will be poured into your lap. For with the measure you use, it will be measured to you." Friends, the more you give, the more God will bless you with; even if it's your last, give and trust God to do the rest.

It is so important that we strive to trust God and put God first in every area of our lives. If you begin to trust God and believe that He is sovereign over your life, you will begin to experience the supernatural; I mean things that are *unexplainable*. I'm telling you this from experience! Many doors have opened, new relationships have been birthed, and money has been chasing me down for a change. My life is simply a breeze, not because I don't have troubles anymore, but because I trust and allow God to lead my life and to fight all my battles.

Constant prayer throughout the day is a large part of your armor. You must stay in God's presence by thanking him constantly and meditating to ensure that you are opening yourself to understanding what God is doing in your life. Often, we do not see what's happening right away, but I assure you if you don't give up, you will see the puzzle come together. Faith without works is dead; you can't just stand still, do nothing, and expect good things. In life, you will have to trust God, be alert, and always be prayerful. Remember, the more you pray, the more God will reveal himself to you. You will start to see things that you would have never have seen without the help of God.

Putting on God's armor also begins with resisting temptation. We must recognize and make every attempt to overcome worldly temptation. Even Jesus was tempted – more than any of us, temptation is not a sin at all, but falling into negative situations is a sin. We are all sinners, and sometimes we will fall short, but the key is to get up, ask God for forgiveness, repent, and try again. People feel guilt and shame, that's the part that keeps us in bondage, we serve a forgiving God who don't allow the devil to trick you into believing you are lesser than anyone else. God loves us all and will forgive us as many times as we ask; the price for our sins have already been paid for, when Jesus died on the cross.

You *will* be tempted. I am still tempted - yes, even after all the fasting, praying daily, church, Bible study, and so on, but I try to catch it and pray about it as soon as possible. I know the blessings that God will pour into our lives if we are obedient because I am a walking example. There is no lack and no failures in the kingdom of God. Doesn't that sound amazing? If only we do the right thing, we can really live a life of freedom, happiness, success, joy, and abundant blessings. If you really think about it, your desire to really live should overtake your desire to sin. Think about how amazing your future would be if you start right now.

Pray daily, stay mindful, meditate, and pray for others. You can whisper to God throughout the day. You can silently talk to Him during a meeting. You can call upon His name whenever and however needed. God is with you everywhere and He hears all prayers.

SETTING GOALS WITH GOD

✦

YOU MAY ASK YOURSELF what does goals have to do with my "Go "moment. The answer to that question is simple; it has *everything* to do with it. Without goals, you are simply wandering in circles. You can't know where you are going without knowing where you are now and where you want to go. We must set specific short and long-term goals.

Goals give you a clear sense of direction and help you to understand more clearly what you want to accomplish. You can have all the potential in the world, but without focus, your abilities and talent are useless. You can't hear God's "Go" moment if you are too busy drifting through life without direction. When you pray for direction, God will show you. He will show you his plans for your life. It may not be the goals you want but God's goals are always best. You can achieve anything in life, if you put your mind to it. We were born to win and to live an abundant life. By setting goals for yourself, you give yourself a target to aim for.

This sense of direction is what allows your mind to focus, rather than waste energy shooting at random.

By setting goals, you give yourself mental boundaries; keeping you focused when distractions pop up. You will not move yourself forward if you have no reason to, for a goal to be effective, it must affect change. No one gets in a car to drive aimlessly to a new town. No, what usually happens is you have directions or your car's GPS on to guide you to your destination. The "Go" moment is knowing the name of the town you need to get to. The rule of thumb is to invite God into your life and follow the plan that he will reveal to you. By following God's plan you are more likely to succeed and you also see your goals and plans manifest through the eye of the Creator.

No one taught me how to set goals. I had mentors talk to me about my goals or the importance of having goals, but the A to Z of the goal setting, was always left out. I want my audience to know how to set goals and how to reach those goals. Goal setting is a powerful process for thinking about your ideal future, and for motivating yourself to turn your vision into reality. The process of setting goals helps you choose where you want to go in life. It literally is giving into your "Go" moment from God with the idea of moving forward towards success. Goals remind you that you are working towards a better life ahead, regardless if the better life is to become a business owner, to be a better parent, to become financially free, or to just straight out win.

By setting sharp, clearly defined goals, you can measure and take pride in the achievement of your progress and you'll see results in what might previously have seemed a long pointless grind. Your goals usually must be defined by what it is you want to work on in life. For me, my "Go" moment was always trying to do everything all at once, I was overwhelmed by all the areas I had to work on and wanted to do it fast. What I have learned is how to do a little bit at a time; Rome wasn't built in a day and the tallest buildings in the world were built a little at a time, thinking about it that way has taught me how to set goals and enjoy the journey.

Ask yourself what you want to do in life? Who do you desire to help? What type of income would you like to see yourself making, how much do you want to earn, by what stage? What are your spiritual goals? Define what you want to acquire, set long and short-term goals. What are the resources you'll need? Who are the people that will help you meet your goals? You need to think about these things and always ask God for clarity.

Next, let's talk a little bit about the family members who are sometimes the worst people to depend on or share our goals with. This is often a difficult subject when thinking about goals because we tend to want to make our family members happy. If you don't put your needs first, you will end up resenting your family for holding you back when it comes to your "Go" moment. Ask yourself if you want to be a parent? If so, how are you going to be a *good* parent? How do you want to be seen by a partner and by members of your extended family? If you are a parent, ask yourself, are you a great parent or do you think you can use some self-development? We can all use a little self-development from time to time. Some things you can never get enough of.

Finally, ask yourself about your attitude. This is huge. If you have a bad attitude, you can set all the goals you want; they are going to be anything more than empty promises. You must *believe* what you say and think. If you say negative things, you are planting negative seeds that result in negative things. If you say positive things, you will gain positive results. You must treat everyone in a Godly fashion and this includes yourself. When it comes to your attitude, ask yourself if there is any part of your mindset holding you back? Remember, you *must* be honest with yourself.

When you ask yourself the above questions, you start to realize the change that is needed in your life and how important setting goals is to help create this change. I pray a lot. And when I started on my journey and received my "Go" moment, there were times that the Holy Spirit told me to simply be still and examine myself. This was my spiritual cleansing, a personal fasting of sorts. It was during this time that I had to create what I call my Destiny mission statement for myself, and I followed it up with the goals needed to work towards what was put in my heart.

My destiny mission statement is something I put in writing to help me understand what God wanted me to do. My destiny mission statement helped me to stay focused on my goals, keeping them at the center of my mind. It also helped me to focus on God, have faith, and live without fear. Creating a destiny mission statement also helped me overcome my temptations and distractions because my WHY became so much more powerful. Without this focus, you can be distracted, or you can spread your effort too thinly across too many things that would get you no closer to your goals. You surely don't want to find yourself with no sharp vision. The Bible tells us where there is no vision; the people perish, (Proverbs 29:18). I love this scripture.

Once you've created your destiny mission statement, taking the time to pray -asking God for his plan for your life- listen for the who and why, then it is time to meditate and wait on God for answers. Never be in a rush to do things the way you know how; God's plans are far greater than we can ever imagine.

You can start this process by stating a positive statement about the goal. The point is to state each goal with a positive tone and without referring to past mistakes. You also want to make sure you use as much attention and detail in the goal's description as possible. "New job" isn't enough, for example. You would want to make a specific goal like "find a new job that allows me to serve others in the medical field and use my degree." You want to be precise about everything from the goal itself to putting in dates and times, so you can measure achievement.

If you are going to give yourself more than one goal, make sure you set priorities. I can tell you firsthand that when you have several goals, you must give each a priority, otherwise it is like having a bunch of notes in your iPhone without any alerts or updates, hence the notes just sit there, waiting for your attention and review. Priorities will help you to avoid feeling overwhelmed by having too many goals or from not paying attention to certain goals, beyond writing them down, at all.

Goal setting is as psychologically important in business as it is in personal life. Are you ready to be a person who goes after it? Are you ready to be someone who values not only yourself, but the gift of God's

"Go" moment, enough that you are prepared to have a growth mindset versus a stunted or victimized mindset? Growing means goals. Going means goals. You can't grow or go without goals. You must set ambitious standards for yourself and have ways to keep yourself accountable. Growing with a destiny mission statement and acting by setting goals is a way to push yourself forward. It is very hard; trust me, I know. You can do this. God is with you. If He brought you to it, He will bring you through it. Don't just Go through it; Grow through it.

I remember reading, "A goal defines an outcome you want to achieve; an area of focus establishes activities you want to spend your time doing," from a piece in the Harvard Business Review. The article went on to say that setting a goal points to a future that you intend to reach. You help yourself become unstuck from who you are while growing into who you are meant to become. Is it hard? Yes, you must reprogram your mind, and ask God to give you a new way of thinking; it takes discipline, it takes obedience, it's challenging work, but it's worth it in the end. Think of it this way; deny your flesh now for a future life of freedom, happiness, joy, and peace.

"Now listen, you who say, 'Today or tomorrow we will go to this or that city, spend a year there, carry on business and make money.' Why, you do not even know what will happen tomorrow. What is your life? You are a mist that appears for a little while and then vanishes" (James 4:13-14). The Bible has verse after verse indicting the value of setting goals. What you must ask yourself is why you have failed to value your own time and talents in the past. Then, you act on moving forward, starting right now. This is your writing on the wall. This is your opportunity to make a fresh start and change, *today*.

You want to look back and know that you did great in life. Your "Go" moment will cause discomfort. Mine led to me leaving my hometown, my family, a lot of materialistic things, and starting my life all over. You may not understand it now, but trust in God and believe that everything happens for a reason. Enjoy the journey; you can do this! If I can, you can.

GWENNETTA WRIGHT,

Serial Entrepreneur / 10 Year Tax Business Expert

AUTHOR AND AWARD-WINNING business owner, Gwennetta Wright, reflects success and diversity within the business landscape. Gwennetta has solidified her role as a serial entrepreneur. With a strong background as a Tax Professional; she utilizes her resources and talents to empower others.

Gwennetta Wright is the owner and developer of Xpert Tax Service LLC, Xpert Business Solutions, and CEO of Reach 4 Your Dreamz Inc. Some of her accolades include receiving the Atlanta Woman of the Week award, as well as winning the Tenacious Business of the Year for Xpert Tax Service (The Greater Columbus Minority Chambers of Commerce, 2011), Small Business of the Year (Firm Grip Organization 2012, 2013), and Community Service Award.

On When God told her to "Go"

My whole career, the last ten years, has been obedient to God. My financial success and being able to expand is all because of God and my relationship with Him. I've been awarded different milestones and accolades in the community, but they don't belong to me; they are property of God. Nothing I do is ever from a place of doing it for the award.

When I look at things from a business perspective, they make sense. But sometimes I get a dream or a vision in my head, which often doesn't make sense, but I do it anyway. That's where God separated me the businesswoman and me the woman of faith. If there is a vision in my head about something, I know God put it there, and I will pursue it regardless of the risk, the odds for success, or what others may advise. The journey, and all of my failures, have taught me so much. At the end of the day, everything comes down to being obedient and your faith.

For people reading right now, *faith is key*. Think about this. I left a steady job to become self-employed. If I look back on the decision from a business perspective, it was a bad decision. The numbers and the risk were not in my favor. God put the vision in my head. He was the one who said, "Go" and gave me the daily strength to work to make it on my own. If I didn't believe in God and know where that vision came from, I wouldn't have the courage to act upon it.

Being observant and being brave are needed when seeking out a Go moment. I once heard that fear and opportunity are the same word in the Japanese language. I'm here to witness that with God, this is true. We don't grow without growing pains. Being fearful but acting upon the opportunities God provides to you is how you reflect faith. My story has always been one of someone who was up against the odds. I had to pray and have faith because everything else about every vision I ever had was a mountain that needed to be moved in order for things to work out.

My biggest external challenge when it comes to my faith and walking in those "Go" moments is getting backlash from those around me. People say I have an attitude sometimes, because I don't accept no or can't as options. When God gives me a vision, he has given me a vision. There is no denying that purpose he has placed in my heart.

What people don't realize is the reason *why* I come off as controlling sometimes, or maybe with an attitude. People around me are not going to understand what I am doing because my vision from God isn't always shared with them. What I am doing doesn't make sense to outsiders who may be looking in and judging while not knowing the full story. What people say about me is only their opinion and sometimes it is the evil one talking or trying to distract me. What I *am* responsible for is making sure God is happy with me and that I listen to his "Go" whenever it is presented to me.

Making people understand why I must do something is a big challenge and sometimes I don't even accept the challenge but rather move forward in spite of what is being said about me.

People care too much about the opinions of others. What they need to care about is their journey and what God is guiding them to do. Being successful boils down to serving others, doing what God has called you to do, and of course, being obedient. It's not always about how much money you can make, but how many others are you helping?

How many people are you showing love to? Put aside the thoughts of caring what others say or think about you. Put aside the doubt, the worry, the fear, and disbelief. There is a video on the Internet right now, portraying the biggest regrets of the elderly and the dying. Most of the time these regrets are about what people didn't do, instead of what they did do. This fact made an impact on me because God gives us gifts, talent, and a vision. When we ignore these gifts, talents, and vision; we are ignoring God's direction for our lives.

God's "Go moment" for you may not make sense in the beginning, but that's okay, you aren't meant to see the end from the beginning, which is why we must totally depend on God to lead and direct our paths. We were not created to go at things alone. Those details will all fall into place with God's time, as long as you remain faithful and obedient.

What I do want to tell people is that prayer is number one when it comes to anything in life. As a businessperson, I have had to struggle a lot. You have highs and lows in business and there are unbelievable pressures in place when you take on the awesome responsibility of writing your own paycheck and the payroll of other people. I pray for help to move me past that overwhelmed feeling. I pray to remind myself that God is in control and the purpose and vision he planted in my head is the prize I have to keep my eye on.

You have to talk to and build a relationship with God in order to be assigned a "Go" moment. There is no question about this. When you know God is on your side, it is easy to get out of the bottomless feelings of doubt and fear.

Planes take off against the wind. Bees fly in spite of science that proves they shouldn't. I have succeeded when I shouldn't have. If you're weary, and a survivor of past failures, know that you are not alone and God is not done with you. The impossible always has an exception to the rule!

No one ever thought I was going to be successful, but because of my faith and always praying God showed up in my life. Never let anyone tell you what you can or can't do. God uses the ones that people dismiss as an example to lift up the next person who may be up against the odds.

God is everything and he has brought me so far, which is why praying and trusting him is so important to me. When you're against all odds, the best thing you can do is keep on going. Your time is near, stand on God's promises. We instinctively want to survive and fight for what we think we have or what we think we want. It is when we take off the gloves and give up on trying to fight our own battles that God steps in and tells us to "Go".

As I sit back and think, I was the girl that people thought would end up being the total opposite of what I am today. All I can say is But God! He always gave me visions; I began to focus on the how instead of the can't. My prayer guided me and the Lord walked alongside me. I started to defy the odds. I took off against the wind. I flew.

I don't work for anyone but myself these days, and I focus on lifting others up. My businesses purposely reach out to touch the lives of others. This is part of my "Go" moment. I realize the blessing in being able to help others discover their gifts and talents. I have learned that God created us to love all, help others, and trust Him.

There were times of great grace when God sent someone of faith to lean in and touch my life in a positive way. Those were moments of clarity and motivation for me. I pay forward those moments by giving back. I reach back and I lift up. I look for those who are weary or have been told "no" and I help them reaffirm, not cut out, what visions have been put in their hearts.

Everything we go through that is perceived as a struggle is either a test of our faith or an opportunity for us to grow, or both. It wasn't until I matured in my faith that I started to realize the weight of the saying "to the one much is given, much is expected." I was being prepared for something when people doubted my ability and my dreams. I had to allow God to work in my life.

If you're in a place of stillness, please know that it is OK. It is not that God has forgotten you or that you don't have enough faith, haven't pray hard enough, or that life is unfair. What comes with stillness is preparation. When things are not working out, when your feet are in the fire, God is getting ready to push you towards your purpose.

It is important to remember that we will not always understand God's plans for us. We have to have faith and trust in Him. Think of these "Go" moments like leaving home without your smartphone. You trust your God-given instinct and spiritual nudges to get you from A to B, without understanding the directions or being able to use GPS to find your path.

It is within my power to share how God has touched my life. I owe everything I have to Him and His "Go" moments. When other people think that life is overpowering or that they are in control, I can't help but preach my testimony. God is always in control, and when you dare to listen to him and go where he leads, you will have everything you need and success *will* find you.

NICOLE STOLL,

⊹⊱✕⊰⊹

Business Executive for Daymond John

NICOLE STOLL SITS IN the Executive office for The Shark Group, and works alongside of celebrity businessman and branding expert Daymond John, the CEO and Founder of FUBU, a $6 billion fashion game-changer.

On When God told her to "Go"

Over the past twenty years, my career has had its share of highs and lows.   I have had the privilege of working with and for the absolute best of the best when it comes to talent. Spike Lee, Sean Combs, Vince McMahon, and Steven Spielberg are some of the notable talent I worked alongside of and was employed by.

While meandering my way through jobs in my early 20's, I bumped into my passion. I couldn't tell you what I wanted for a career, but I knew I loved music; it was that love of music led me on the road towards my

56

"Go" moment with God. There were all these little steps that led me from working in and around music to working for one of the most successful entrepreneurs in the world. This success led me to eventually walking away from it all to start my business, Just Brilliant.

When I started to get into music, I was 22 and I was working in the A&R department at a record label. I wanted to be behind the scenes and be part of the process that contributed to making music; I wanted to tell stories and be creative.

This was the "first love" medium and it was instrumental in getting me to where I am today. Back then, I wasn't really working with direction, but I knew what I loved and I knew it was a blessing to not only love what you did but also get paid for it. It was an electrifying feeling, but there was still something missing. I loved what I did, but it wasn't fulfilling. It wasn't my purpose. It didn't feel valuable, as though it offered any real contribution.

As I started to seek out more fulfilling uses for my talent, I began to listen for what God had to say to me and the direction He was pointing me in. I have always been a spiritual person and someone who walks with faith on a minute-to-minute basis (I even pray for parking and good hair days). I pray for and about everything.

People may find it a little hard to understand when I state that God is my Father and he blesses my decisions and my direction in life (when I'm obedient, and sometimes even when I'm not). I say this to explain that He comes to me as a still small voice. He puts in and on my heart; quite often it bubbles under the surface and makes itself clear to me.

For example, I may be in prayer about something and be in constant conversation with the Father about it for direction. I will get to a place where I feel unsure and if I speak out loud to someone in fellowship, I would hear precisely what is been being said to me.

How people look to their earthly father as whom they want to be, this is how I look to God- as my father. I question whom I should date, who I should be friends with, and I pray for continued direction in my career, my personal growth, legacy on earth, and fulfilling his purpose for me. And when I am feeling challenged, I talk to him and ask for answers. I ask for signs that I can't miss. For those little nudges, remember that it is the nudges that will lead you in the direction the Father wants you to go.

Asking God to tell you where to go will not always give you the answer you want. One of these "Go" moments came when I was shown it was time to walk away from a successful career, in a position that offered amazing potential and incredible access for growth. My last position was as the right hand to Daymond John, the founder of FUBU and star of Emmy award-winning business reality television show, Shark Tank. Essentially, I was responsible for his day-to-day business affairs, as well as some of his private concerns. It was a round the clock type of situation. There was so much to be done that I couldn't always hear my own voice.

I was also dealing with challenges in my personal life. I was blessed with a child, but the situation wasn't ideal. I had made a permanent decision with a temporary person. The challenge was real and I needed to pray about my situation and where I was in life, both personally and professionally.

These were conversations that I had in my head and times when I spoke out loud to God. It was more conversation. I want this emphasized. When I prayed, I was *literally* talking to God. I was thinking out loud and listening back. When I became pregnant, it was time for things to change. My focus was no longer on myself, but now on my child first and foremost. I had to examine everything that was put before me by God and think about the future. Where God was leading me, and where I was headed, felt like two different journeys.

I found myself with two amazingly blessed situations before me. Truthfully; to whom much is given, much is required, and it is never a simple choice.

My child is a gift; who needed me and deserved focus and my attention. At the same time, I had a wonderful career, with people who depended on me, and I that had a responsibility to. I owed both of them my very best self. My child deserved more, as did my boss. I decided to leave my job. It was what God was telling me to do; it was my "Go" moment.

There came a period of time when I struggled with what I knew had to be done and actually doing the deed. I wanted to have it all. I would pray for an answer and then become frustrated because I kept getting the same response from God. I did everything I could to delay the "Go", but I knew it was coming. God was hinting at what I needed to be done. I was trying my best to ignore it.

One day, I woke up in an amazing apartment, in a renowned location, with the pressure of trying to manage my professional life and maintain my personal one. I was suffocating. I was overloaded. Neither my boss nor my daughter was getting what they deserved from me.

I had been in constant conversation with God. I had what people call a "real job", with a boss whom I loved and respected, but I also had a child, who I needed to parent and love.

The conversations with God were many and I continually fought his directive. Still, I understood my

"Go" moment couldn't be delayed any longer. I packed up my house and put everything on a moving truck. I moved to Atlanta with no job, no car, no place to live, and leaving most of my family and friends behind. I walked away from a career that others would fight so hard to get, but this is what God had put in my heart, and I had to honor Him by being obedient.

My faith is punctuated by being obedient; to what I believe the Father is telling me. Every decision I have made, or sometimes the decisions he has made for me, have made me who I am. You always have the challenge of submitting when it comes to "Go. As you're reading this, the steps seem easy, but you may find yourself doubting what you have been told. It won't always make sense. It often won't be comfortable. You may not want to listen or you may try getting around it. That is a waste. God has a huge plan for us all. Most of the time the "hints", the "uneasiness" in a situation, the small growing feeling that you can or should be doing more or less is what will lead you to "Go".

You may have the challenge of controlling your pride. Pride gets in our way on many things and it is an unfortunate part of the human condition. I have had issues with pride, but I struggled with fear more than pride. This is where my faith comes in. Faith is your safety net. When you're obedient and you step out, faith is there to make sure you don't fall.

My biggest challenge when God has told me to "Go" has been my own insecurity. I happened to be blessed with a wonderful circle of people around me. Going forward, remember that some people rely on their pride, and it is these people who will be disobedient to God. Their pride will create their fall. Having faith will always put you in the right place, at the right time. Trust the "Go" from God in your life and you will find yourself surrounded with the right people   at   the   right   time.

PRIDE DOESN'T PASS GO

THE FOUNDATION OF THE Bible and witness accounts of "Go" moments have been laid out for you in the chapters thus far. I still have another powerful "Go" story that I will share later in the book, but I want to use this chapter talk further about the disease of pride. The thing about pride is we usually don't realize we are impacted by it until we have really hit rock bottom. Pride is a deadly disease. Each day I pray to God to remove every single ounce of pride, did you know God won't show mercy and favor to a person who is full of pride? Pride would have us so lost and stupid. The devil is the epitome of using pride to destroy us.

In business, as in your personal life, you will battle with pride. It will either be your pride or someone else's, but the ego, evil, and hindrances caused by pride will always be around you. This is something you will have to meditate on and pray about on a daily basis.

The kind of pride that prevents you from experiencing a "Go" moment is a sin in my eyes. People usually have trouble reaching goals and pursuing dreams because they are too prideful to risk appearing "stupid." Pride also convinces people that they've already done enough, and from this, I have found they experience a sense of entitlement. Pride causes people to blame others for their lack of success, which is never the case. *You* are responsible for your own life. If you worry about your circumstances, or what someone else is doing to you, then you can't trust God. Your pride is in the way!

Pride is universally defined as a feeling of deep pleasure or satisfaction derived from one's own achievements, the achievements of those with whom one is closely associated, or from qualities or possessions that are widely admired. But false pride exists too. People take credit for achievements they didn't or couldn't accomplish on their own. Or, in many cases, they latch on to glitter.

I consider "latching on to glitter" a prominent practice in the entertainment field. I work within its scope and I see this all the time. For example, someone may bump into Celebrity Joe Blow in an elevator and suddenly there is a selfie and a claim that they worked together. Not only is this lying, but it is also usually pride-based lying.

Pride causes problems to get bigger, last longer, grow louder and more concrete challenges within families. There is nothing about pride that is aligned with God's will. How we treat people and how we conduct ourselves should always be within the Will of God and not based within our own pride.

When I was praying about my "Go", a few weeks before my wreck, my pride was a big issue. It looked like everything was okay from the outside but I wasn't, I was in a deep mess. I had so much debt, I had so many liabilities, I was buried in what I thought was success; little did I realize I was failing miserably spiritually and emotionally. There were many things going wrong in my life and my pride was not allowing me to break down so I could break through.

Pride was holding me back from accepting what God had in store for me. If I didn't have so much pride, I would have inherited the gifts He had in store for me today a lot sooner, and with a lot less heartache. We all learn lessons at our own pace. Pride is a lesson and we all have moments where we are schooled.

When I started ThinkZILLA, my pride was boiling over. I knew I had the drive and the experience. I felt like I could accomplish everything by myself. I wasn't going to ask anyone for anything. Pride will make you suffer in silence. Pride will harm your connection with God. Pride causes you to be disillusioned with a quality of life and more focused on labels, brands, societal associations, and status; things that don't truly matter. When you are in need, pride will keep you from reaching out to others who can uplift you, offer you guidance, or even simply hold hands and pray with you. I honestly believe pride is the tool of the evil one.

Prideful people like to appear as if they have everything figured out. They are terrified of being wrong or, worse, they are afraid of appearing vulnerable. These fears put them on dangerous ground, because those people won't ask for help, they won't ask questions, and they don't want to do anything to challenge the status quo.

There were moments in my early ThinkZILLA days when I bought into my own pride. We all experience this buy-in on a small level at one time or another. Maybe you find a great hair stylist and spend some extra time in the mirror upon arriving home admiring yourself, but what happens when the need to be the best-looking or the smartest or the richest or the one with the most designer clothes and the most expensive car leads you to become lost in translation within your own life?

Pride is not only a sin, but pride steals away your purpose and your voice. When you are full of pride, it is hard to ask for help. It is even harder to ask for forgiveness. How can you repent for your sins or say you are sorry for hurting someone when you are full of pride? How can you accept God's "Go" when you think you know it all or that you are in control of your life and your destiny?

Pride is a disease. Think about this. What is the definition of disease? It is defined as a condition of the living animal or plant body or of one of its parts that impairs normal functioning and is typically manifested by distinguishing signs and symptoms.

When you sit and pray about your pride, ask yourself about your compassion. When I was caught up in my pride, like thinking I could fix all my problems, I was standing in my own way. I was struggling to breath and yet choking myself at the same time. I was filling my life's void not with a relationship with God, but with things that looked good or made me temporarily feel good.

As you have already learned in the stories shared prior to this chapter, obedience is key. You can't be prideful and obedient to God at the same time. It doesn't work. We all slip up and we all fall into traps of pride. With God's help, and compassion for ourselves, we can retrain our spirit and our self-love, as well as love for others, to squash pride and celebrate God's hand in our lives.

There is a great story titled, The Scarlet Ibis by James Hurst. The story is told from the narration of a character we only come to know as "Brother". He frankly talks about his brother, Doodle, and his disability. His pride limits his ability to empathize with Doodle. He repeatedly tries to make Doodle able-bodied for his own benefit. Eventually, "Brother" causes Doodle's death. The damage pride can cause in a life is well illustrated in The Scarlet Ibis.

I couldn't "Go" until I put my pride aside. I had to be willing to listen and more willing to be obedient. I had to be honest and open with myself and with God. I had to admit to my failures, confess my sins, and - the worst thing for someone suffering from the disease known as pride- ask for help and guidance.

We can't know what we don't know. You will only get so far, faking your way through life, pretending to have it all figured out. You are not meant to live this life as a self-guided tour. This life is to be a journey of lessons with the guidance of God. Pride causes prolonged suffering; the more we succumb to our own pride, the harder it is to spot and address the suffering.

Ask yourself where you are right now. What is important to you? What is holding you back? Are you able to afford everything you have? Do you have needless material things that you can't afford? Do you have self-compassion and empathy for others? Have you been afraid to start that honest conversation with

God about where you are when you are low or why you avoid deep prayer?

Pride is also an attempt to please everyone. Guess what? You can't please everyone. There is an old story about a man who is walking into town with his grandson and a donkey. He walks by a window and overhears a woman say that the man is stupid because he isn't letting the small child sit on the donkey. So, the man puts the child on the donkey. Next, the man walks by another woman's window that says that the child is selfish not to let the old man ride the donkey. The man removes the child and climbs onto the donkey. Finally, the man rides into town on the donkey and someone asks him why he isn't allowing the child to ride the donkey and why is he making the child walk. The point is you will never win every client. You will never gain every success. And, you will never have the approval of every person. Your pride will try to make you think, however, that you *can* earn everyone's approval.

Think about yourself from a place motivated by envy. In many cases, envy and pride can be defined as the same thing, but from a different point of view. Envy can cause you to become disenfranchised, greedy, and selfish in an attempt to gain material things, not experiences with other people or a relationship with God.

What I have learned about my car accident miracle is that nothing is more precious in life than life itself. The old me, including material things I had in my past, is gone and I couldn't be happier. Now, this doesn't mean you and I don't deserve nice things. We do, but they shouldn't be the primary focus of our life's purpose or the "why" behind the goal. God's Will for our lives should always be number one as far as focus and the "why" behind how we conduct ourselves.

Envy and the disease of pride are not only Christian problems, but *human* problems. Regardless of our cultural or spiritual backgrounds, psychologists from around the world all agree that pride and envy are negative components and motivators within our lives and things that hold us back.

Because pride can ruin relationships, and destroys sensations, emotions, and people, psychologist have composed article after article about how to cope with, and even overcome, pride. One psychologist even penned a blog stating, "it seems truly dangerous to because we can all fall into its claws, for it is so far extended that it has reached the level of a pandemic." The word pandemic is never used lightly. With all the selfies and "me-centric" branding going on in the world of business, how can we avoid the pitfall of this prideful pandemic; especially if God is not number one in our life? The question is interesting and remains unanswered.

I know, in my specific situation, that relying upon God was the only way I was going to give up my pride to become completely submissive to God. I think when you look behind the curse of envy, and its negative language, such as gossip; you will notice that envy hides a terrible demon that does not take pity on us. This is called a lack of self-esteem and self-love.

Envy also tempts us into making comparisons between ourselves and others, which suffocates us in a blanket of unrealistic expectations that are usually completely off course from where God wants us to be! It is widely known that comparison is harmful, as it causes us to fixate on our shortcomings and frustrations. Envy also mutes God's "Go" moments, distracting us from the achievement of dreams, while also preventing us from seeing what we already possess.

For me, it was always easier to channel frustration into judgment and criticism than to recognize my own shortcomings and inferiorities. If things were not going my way, it was always someone else's fault. I wasn't allowing myself to grow. I wasn't willing to find and address challenges within my own life, which is the biggest symptom of the disease of pride/envy.

Pride is a disease. It can wreck your life. It can harm a marriage. It can cause you to make a bad decision because you become so focused on you that you tune out God's "Go". This is something that you must ask God to help you with; learn to talk to God like your best friend, I promise you he will answer your prayers. God will open your heart and mind by working on the wounds to repair the soul.

BUSINESS & SUCCESS;

Why Matthew 6:33 Matters

"**B**UT SEEK FIRST HIS kingdom and his righteousness, and all these things will be given to you as well."- Matthew 6:33

Here is a part of my deep, dirty, and dark secret - at one point in my life, I was in such distress that I was running my business on faith alone; it seemed like everyone turned their back on me - even my family. I could not access cash or credit. My bank accounts were literally frozen with money my clients had paid me for work that was due or coming due.

I found myself backed into a corner. And, again, I got there because of my pride. I couldn't admit to being in trouble and facing the issues I had, which were minor mistakes any young, successful person making $100k a year could make. Not only was I in a place of now having to work essentially for free, but there was no way of paying my bills or buying gas or groceries.

As you may have already read, the "Go" doesn't always come at the best time. Like in the ladies' stories in the previous chapters, the "Go" came at a needed time of growth, not at a time of convenience. I had to uproot everything I had so I could "Go" and when I got to where I needed to be, I still had to output work for clients who had already paid me. I was under tremendous pressure and stress.

When I was in my early twenties, working for Google and in the collections business, how I handled my business was not in the way of seeking the kingdom of righteousness. I was really caught up with ego and pride and almost consumed with money. My first priority wasn't God; it was money - which turned out to be a huge mistake.

I write this now because it is vitally important for entrepreneurs of every age to understand how to prioritize their business mission and endeavors when they first start out. Putting God at the top of your life is the best thing you can do. With every effort, you want to put God first, so you can work forward towards the life God wants to give you, those Destiny genes that are inside each of us.

If you focus on things like how much money you will make, then intention to serve God gets put on the back burner, because your main priority and idol is money. I always tell people that if you follow your purpose the money will chase you down. That's very important, and isn't it a great thing to know that if you are working and living in purpose God will give you more than you can ever imagine having. I know its very hard to have that thought process but its true. You must trust God in every area of your life. I remember the time when I did put money first, the business never lasted. God was on the back burner in my life then, even though I thought I was honoring God, I wasn't. God sits and wait on us to surrender and trust him and the longer we take to do so, the worse things get and we don't really realize it until we are dead broke and confused.

When I finally had my "Go" my relationship with God grew stronger because I was forced to trust in His will. Letting go of where we think we are headed and obeying God is a challenge, but I promise the most enriching moments of your life will follow.

God should be the center of everything; I don't make any decisions if God is not in the midst of them. You can't thrive as a human being if your focus isn't right. My company in the beginning took on corporate clients, hip hop clients, boxers, whoever needed help, but I began working with a lot of religious-based clients. That was truly God's plan; it surely wasn't my own. I didn't think I was good enough to work with churches, but God used me just the way I was. And it helped me grow into the person I've become today. Did I think of myself as a "bad" Christian? No. I have always loved God and thought I dedicated myself to him. But, I - like most humans- had downfalls.

I tell people all the time to do what they love, so they will never have to work a day in their life. When you do what you are called to do and love to do, it doesn't really feel like work. I love helping people build their brands and bringing people's visions into reality. I can literally do it in my sleep; God has given us all unique gifts and talents, things that we do very well. I thank God that I have found my niche and purpose in life.

God has used me to do some amazing things for people, and he will use you too, to do amazing things in the lives of others. There are people with severe disabilities who must fight stereotypes, bullying, comprehension issues, lesser pay issues, and so much more. But they simply play the cards they are dealt. I know some people that complain all day and have everything they need to change their situations, but yet their mind is not in the right place.

What do we do as able-bodied people? We make memes about Mondays. We get political and we backstab. We focus on bonuses and paychecks, and complain about opportunities we fought so hard for. We're not putting God first when we do this. We are not serving each other, His mission, or ourselves. We are lost sheep in need of guidance.

When I found myself at a gas station needing fuel with a frozen bank account that reflected a large amount of money that I couldn't touch, I knew God was trying to get my attention. I was humbled by my mistakes and I was forced to reexamine my intentions, both personally and professionally.

I had some things I needed to work out as far as how I conducted myself as a child of God. I saw this because it's so easy to get lost in business. We can let our direction change in a moment by engaging in gossip, thinking that we are in control, by having pride, by hanging with people we should not, and by going places we have no business going. Until we take accountability for our actions, we will go nowhere.

One of my favorite passages on GotQuestions.org relates to seeking the kingdom of God. The popular website reads, "God has promised to provide for His own, supplying every need (Philippians 4:19), but His idea of what we need is often different from ours, and His timing will only occasionally meet our expectations. For example, we may see our need as riches or advancement, but perhaps God knows that what truly we need is a time of poverty, loss or solitude."

God knows what we need will always be different than what we think we need and what we are working for. I was working for me, not for God. God knocked on my door several times. God took away everything so I could focus on who I am, my purpose in life and what I needed to do to reset my life; even now, telling my story to the world. I know this book will change so the lives of many people.

Integrity and Matthew 6:33 really do play upon each other, too. If you're out there right now reading this book with a dream in your heart, remember to conduct yourself with integrity. I've learned from my past. I had to admit that I wasn't always working for the kingdom of God, but was working to promote Velma's kingdom, which would be nothing without God!

Consider where you are today with the dream God put in your heart. Are you seeking to do something with it that will uplift and inspire others? Or are you in it for the money? Fame? Societal success? We should be more careful about how we consider moving forward with business dreams because we will always find ourselves having to work with others who are not yet saved, which means they may not quite understand you, but you must display the spirit of God always. You are always being watched. In fact, you are the only Bible that some people may read.

When I made it to Atlanta, before I headed out on the day that changed my life, I was walking around the house meditating and praying. One thing I did realize is that the Bible and the word of God provides us with everything we need; it's a roadmap. It teaches us how to conduct ourselves, how to treat others, what to do and not do. It even teaches us to seek wisdom, knowledge and discernment, which is the foundation of everything.

I started to rebuild my life in my head and I did the same with my business too. The Bible also teaches about conflict. Think about it, there are a lot of conflicting opinions in the Bible. People doubted the disciples. There were social issues with the woman at the well. People loathed the tax collectors. There was a lot of business going on in the Bible. To this day, people debate about what certain stories in the Bible actually mean. Everyone will have their own perception and understanding of what they interpret, so do your homework; read and study your Bible.

There is nothing worse than just listening to what others must say about the Bible, without knowing it yourself; especially nowadays - so many false teachers and prophets. By not reading your Bible, you are at a disadvantage of believing everything you hear. Get to know God yourself. God is waiting on you to seek Him; you don't have to go through a friend or pastor to reach God. You can start where you are with what you have by getting on your knees and seeking Him fully. As with anything you do in life, it is important that you study, learn, and get to know things for yourself. Knowledge is power. We are never too smart to stop learning. In fact, the more we read, the smarter we become.

Over the past few years, I have dedicated much time into reading and listening to self-help material. I have learned that to become a better person, we must start within. And the challenge with that is most people don't see that they have a problem. This is where seeking God became an important part of my daily life. I knew that to become an ambassador for Christ I had to clean myself up first. It's hard to help others before you help yourself. How can you help anyone on an empty spiritual balance?

I always pray to God for a new heart; I pray for restoration and a renewing of my mind. And now my relationship with God is the number one relationship of my life. According to statistics, and some psychologists, it takes 66 days to change a habit. Just like it took time to form the habits, now it will take time to change them. Change is good, and becoming a better version of you is excellent. Who doesn't want to become better? If I can change, I know anyone can.

Does this mean you will never make a mistake or give into temptation? No, but the Holy Spirit will convict you when you are doing wrong. You will understand you can't expect for God to answer your prayers while at the same time disobeying the word of God. Every time I am tempted to do something, I think about how good God have been to me, and how, if I stay on track, so many more blessings will follow me. I also fear the consequences that may come if I do wrong. The bottom line is, I have way too much on the line.

I believe in keeping God at the center of my life, that means in business, my personal life, in my children's life; every area. It is just as easy to do the right thing as it is to do the wrong thing, you can do anything you put your mind to doing. In fact, once you start to live the right type of life, your desires for the wrong things and things you once were attracted to will change.

Think of your life as a testimony of God's work. You are either working to please him or you're not. It's *that* simple. Most people think they can pick and choose what part they want to do right, but there is no grey area. There is no in-between. As I close this chapter, I want to stress how much better you will feel in all areas of your life by developing a relationship with God and by being authentic, intentional, and mindful about spiritual growth and change.

What we learn along the path of our journey is what helps us become better people; it shapes us for what's to come and it allows us to pass along the lessons we learned to others along the way. Working for God is the best position we can have. The good news is that we are all children of God. We are blessed and highly favored, right now. We have everything we need, you can take what you have, and become better. Right now, you must choose if you want a blessed life or just a simple life. I choose a blessed life!

Chose to be grateful, thankful, and intentional going forward. Never allow your mind to consume negativity, change the channel quickly. Always think things that are positive, honest, empowering, and hopeful. Learn to stop yourself each time you get ready to complain; that is the greatest trick of the devil, to get you to think about what you may have lost and even push you into self-pity.

I have since discovered that none of the material things amount to anything if you don't have God. Like the song says, "I'd rather have Jesus than silver and gold". Now here is the amazing thing with Jesus, you *can* have silver and gold. In fact, God promises so much that it will cause an overflow. This is my favorite reference scripture, Luke 6:38: "Give, and it will be given to you. A good measure, pressed down, shaken together and running over, will be poured into your lap. For with the measure you use, it will be measured to you."

YOU WILL BE TESTED.

————⋆✦⋆————

PRAY ALWAYS AND continually, always pray. Remember our flesh is weak, and without daily prayer, we can easily fall back into old habits and patterns.

The closer you grow to God, the more you will be tempted. Sounds crazy, right? This is so true. I had all type of crazy temptations when I gave my life to Christ. The devil would whisper things in my mind, like just give up, you're never going to amount to anything, no one loves you or cares about you, go get drunk, go hang out etc. you get the point. You must be strong.

Don't question. Stop worrying. Get real with God.

You will need a spiritual backbone of steel when it comes to defeating the devil. Our fight is not physical; we fight spiritually. And worry is another highly effective trick of the devil. The Bible tells us that we should not worry about what we will eat or what we will wear, but time after time we allow worry to be a downfall. I say repeatedly, it is not easy to follow Christ, which is why the world is so corrupt; it seems easier to sin and do what others are doing. Many are called, but only a few are chosen. To win, you must prepare to win, and prepare yourself for the road ahead. As I stated earlier, the devil won't come with new tricks, they are the same old tricks.

Another trick of the devil is discouragement. The devil thrives on trying to get you looking at your past life, mistakes you've made, sins, weaknesses, and failures! It's hard to get up in the morning and have hope and faith in a world where every time you try to do the right thing, something knocks you down. For me, discouragement was a big one. The devil would always try to tempt me by making me pity myself. I hated that then I would start to compare my life with the lives of others, which just made it worse. I learned quickly to thank God for everything he had blessed me with, and by doing so it allowed me to switch the channels on the discouraging thoughts.

Know that you are a child of God. He created us in His image and He created us differently for a reason, we are who we are for a good reason, flaws and all; no one is perfect. It is impossible to be perfect, in fact, trying to be perfect and error free is a prideful way of thinking. But the more you grow with God and seek him, you become more and more like him; allowing his spirit to live in you.

God will never abandon you because you sin, that's another false myth; a lot of people don't turn to God because they don't think they are perfect enough. God wants to be a part of your life, just as you are, right now. Once you take the first step, God will do the rest. Never allow anyone to make you feel that they are better than you because they know more Bible scriptures than you. You can receive God as your lord and savior just like anyone else, RIGHT NOW!

The devil will try to distract and shake you. I was shaken when God led me to leave Houston; I worried I was making the wrong decision by leaving a place where I was very successful to go into another place where I would have to build and meet new people. There again, I wasn't depending on God, I was still trying to do it myself, which is why I was shaken.

The devil knows how to pick at your weak areas and shortcomings, and he also knows how to exaggerate them and blow all your worries out of proportion! This is also another tactic he uses often. Filling your head with a bunch of lies that seem to be true, he's the master of trickery. He knows that it will be a challenge to get you down if you are connected to God by praying and following God's path. Therefore, I can't stress enough to pray always and continually. Even when you think you're strong enough, you still need to pray. It's a daily battle. It will be harder for the devil to plant things in your mind causing you to lose hope if you will walk with God, take things one day at a time, and pray.

When you pray to God, you must ask God to show you things from a Godly point of view and not your own. Often, we are our own worst enemy. When I pray, I ask God to allow me to see myself the way he sees me. I also ask God to take away the roots of self-doubt, fear, and discouragement. I can honestly say that once I began asking God to change me, he did just that.

Discouragement is a loss of courage, resulting from a lack of faith. The devil will use a lack of faith to back up your human emotions. "Faith comes from hearing the word of God" (Romans 10:17), thus when you feel discouraged, the quickest remedy is to start praying and reciting the Word of God. When I feel the devil trying to creep in my presence, I immediately rebuke it in the name of Jesus, and say, *devil you are a liar!*

Consider what you have learned thus far. It would have been very easy for me to stay in Houston and not follow God's direction. It would have been easy for me to throw my hands in the air and plant in my mind that I would never be successful. Those were the easy options and they looked awfully appealing from the discouragement and odds against me point of view.

I chose to honor God, stand on scripture, have faith, and work hard. I knew my faith would carry me through the fire if I trusted God. I knew I needed change. You may feel like giving up, you may be experiencing financial problems, you may be experiencing serious health problems and feeling doubtful. My word to you right now is God did not bring you this far to leave you. The problems that you are experiencing right now are preparing you for the best part of your life, which is still to come. Do not worry about what will happen next week or even tomorrow, rest in God's presence right now. He is the only person that can help you overcome things.

God allows problems in our life so that we can focus more on him. God has good things in store for you, remember that you must fight and sacrifice to get what God have for you. To whom much is given, much is required. It may be rough right now, but God will see you through it. Stand up, hold your head high, and know that God is with you; he will never leave you. You may even feel alone and feel that God is not with you or for you because of some things that may have happened; you may have lost a loved one, you may be battling cancer or a serious virus, you may have lost your job, you may be going through a divorce, but God *is* right there with you. God is preparing you for the next level in your life; he's preparing you for an amazing future.

When the self-doubt and the temptations start to kick-in, simply whisper God's name and those small acts of faith will bring God closer to you, helping you to get your mind back on the right track. Please understand that we *all* make mistakes; ask God to forgive you, repent, and keep on working at becoming a better version of you. Remember you are the only one that can separate yourself from God. The Bible tells us that Jesus is the same yesterday, today, and forever. Live life, be free, tap into your destiny genes, discover your purpose, always pray, and thank God.

Always be thankful, count your blessings, thank and praise Jesus for all that he has done for you! There is power in prayer, and God smiles when we are grateful, humble, and prayerful. Every day that goes by, I get on my knees and thank God for everything. I thanked God for all my troubles, all my failures, and all my mistakes in life, because without them, I would not be who I am today. I am a walking testimonial for Christ and having a relationship with God is the best thing that could have ever happened to me.

Prayer and meditation is a great spiritual tool to use on a daily basis. Never be afraid to face oppositions in life, it is through those times that you should put all your trust and faith in God. After all, how do you expect to see God's super natural favor in your life if you never surrender and allow him to work? Speaking positive thoughts are another way to resist the devil, let the light of positive words shine brightly into your spirit.

The devil hates songs of prayer and praise to Jesus. Singing hymns through praise and worship is a wonderful way to get into the presence of God. I love to listen to Juanita Bynum, Tasha Cobb, and Marvin Sapp's Praise and Worship YouTube station. I can always count on some great praise and worship music to set the tone of my day and bring me closer to God.

Resist, defy, and attack the Enemy by taking positive action and doing something good, even if it is singing a church song or being of service to someone in need. Your actions will always speak as loud as your positive words and positive words and actions are the best way to counteract evil and negativity within your life.

When you're going through rough times in life, it is happening for a reason. Don't allow it to get you down; God is up to something. God led me out of Houston for a reason, my last relationship ended for a reason, my car totaled, and me telling you my story is for a reason. You must stand strong in your faith. Scripture tells us that faith without works is dead. Life and death is in the power of your tongue. When you pray, meditate, fast, read your Bible, and seek God continually - you will experience a new life.

NICOLE MCCOY,

Accountant & Tax Strategist

GOD IS MY FATHER. He is my Lord. He is my savior. He is the only person I totally depend on. It isn't always like that for everyone, but it should be. People need to hear the stories of how God moved mountains. I have heard people say there is no proof of God. My life is proof of God. I have had things happen to me, divine interventions, that shouldn't have happened. There is no rational explanation for these events. All that exists is the Holy Spirit touching my life.

The biggest "Go" moment came when I was incarcerated. I didn't know why I was locked up when I was first arrested. I didn't know if they had someone else or if someone had pinned something wrongly upon my reputation. I was in shock and upset. I started to pray about it and then I was informed why I was placed in handcuffs and taken to jail.

I learned that I had to pay a penalty on something I did when I was younger. Without getting into the details, I do regret my crime. I wasn't proud of it. I was remorseful and filled with sorrow. I also was scared for who I was and who I could become. There was a part of me who could easily find herself mixed in with the wrong crowd. There is a duality that exists in all of us.

When I was locked up, God came to me. I spoke to myself using silent prayer and internal conversations to get God's attention all of the time. It was during the time I was being held in jail that God decided he was going to give me a "Go" moment. Imagine this, God telling you to "Go" when in jail.

I decided to listen, which was unusual for me. I liked being in charge of who I was and what I was doing. Something was different about how the Holy Spirit was moving through me, however, and I had to really sit back and listen. I had to look at who I was and how I got myself arrested. There were a lot of ugly things about my past that came up during this time, things I did that I didn't want to face.

God told me what he needed from me while I sat and prayed quietly. He wanted me to trust him with my situation. I had to learn to be obedient for once in my life and I think God stepped in at this moment because he knew I could go either way. This stint in jail was meant to be my warning, not a trend in my life.

I went on a fast after God directed me to do so. The other cellmates were in shock. No one could understand how I couldn't be hungry after days of not eating, but I wasn't. In fact, I didn't speak or eat for four days. If God had told me to do the same for forty days I would have done so. It was during the time of fasting that the Holy Spirit put me, not only to the test as far as trust in God was concerned, but he tasked me with reaching out to a dangerous enemy of mine too.

I really felt myself starting to count on God. The night before my court appearance, I looked around the prison cell. I stated this was would be the *last* time I would sleep on that prison bed. This would be the last time someone, other than God, could dictate the limits on my life. My fast was coming to an end and my new life was about to begin.

I woke up the next day and God asked me to "Go" into the bathroom. This was right before I was due into court. The need to walk into the bathroom and fall to my knees was heavy. I wanted to cry and I had an inkling to be mad all at the same time. I was going to go in front of a judge for something that happened years ago. Sometime I was sorry for. Something I regretted.

The time I spent in the bathroom that morning was literally like having the evil one and an angel on my shoulders. It was stereotypical, but it was real. I heard a voice inside me start to question why I was kneeling. I ignored it and started speaking out loud. All I could do was shower God with my praises in advance.

I was told that the fasting was over and that I needed to be thankful for God had showed me what he needed to show me. He had paused my life for a reason and gave me this needed lesson. I was told I would learn from this lesson and go forth to be successful in the world, and that I was not going to be in jail within a few hours. The more I praised Jesus for helping me in my time of need, the more confident I had felt that I was truly experience God's grace and would not be returned to prison after my court appearance.

I went into court on this particular morning and the Holy Spirit used me in a way that I will never forget. A few days prior, there was an incident when I was in the jail. I came into contact with another inmate who had the mark of the beast on her neck. The numbers 666 stood out at me and we just clashed. Her vibe and my vibe were two entirely different things and we had laid hands upon one another.

As I was waiting to go into court, I noticed she was waiting too. We tried not to make eye contact and to ignore each other as much as possible. This is when the

Holy Spirit humbled me and used me. God wanted me to apologize to this inmate for putting my hands on her. Nothing in my DNA wanted this to happen, but when God says, "Go", you have to be obedient and submissive.

I had to humble myself out of obedience for God. I had to remain in the spirit of Thanksgiving and ignore my instincts in order to work out God's will. The Holy Spirit asked me to walk over to her, apologize, and then speak to her. I knew any moment this woman could get violent with me again and that a fight could break out, which wouldn't look good for either of us who were about to stand in front of our peers and a judge.

I trusted God, however, when he told me to go to her. With both hesitation and determination, I approached this particular inmate. I told her I had to apologize because I didn't act towards her in a Christ like manner. I told her as a Christian I was disappointed by my own behavior and that it was not acceptable.

"You're going to go outside and your mother is out there." Those words then came out of my mouth. The inmate with the 666 tattoo started to cry. Words about this woman's personal life flowed out of my mouth and then off of my tongue as if I knew her. The truth is, outside of our physical confrontation, I didn't know her from Eve. The Holy Spirit was speaking through me, perhaps trying to confirm a "Go" moment to her.

"Your mom is outside and you are going to be alone. You will not be released today because God wants to sit you down, in prison, and evaluate who you are and where you have been." I was promising more specifics, someone also sharing her plight.

I couldn't understand where this was coming from, but I knew it was a positive message and I wasn't about to attempt to stop it. She began to cry harder, almost weeping. I told her to apologize to her mother, specifically for hitting and cursing her mom.

Our eyes locked and there was a kinship there. She knew what I was saying was directly from the mouth of God as I had no information about her, her case, her relationship with her mother, or much else, prior to me approaching the woman with the 666 tattoo.

Then, it was my turn to walk into court. I wanted to remain in faith with God, but I have to admit there was a part of my heart that was doubtful. I was also expecting to see my own mother, but she did not show up. She was missing from my life on that court date. Just as I thought I would have to face the music alone, I noticed people from my old job gathered together in the courtroom. They were looking at me not as a judge, but as set of friends who were willing to support me in any way possible. They were acting in the true spirit of Christ.

This is when you have to put on God's armor. I was about to be tested as far as my faith. God had me kneeling in a prison bathroom, thanking him for the miracle of my release. I had every reason to trust in him, especially after the Holy Spirit spoke through me to the woman with the 666 tattoo. But, even with God in my heart and knowing I was obedient to God, including the four-day fast, I still felt trepidation about being released.

I put my head down and I heard someone in the courtroom whisper, "18 months." Then I heard the Holy Spirit say, "You don't trust me?" My doubt was showing. It took a strong internal effort to ignore the negativity and being preyed upon by the evil one. As the Judge looked through my file and spoke with me, I tried not to show any emotions. I tried to stay still and within the light of God. Finally, the Judge said he was going to release. He even said out loud that he didn't know why he was doing this, but he felt an urgency to do so.

Obedience is everything when it comes to your "Go" moments from God. You have to surrender yourself. You will be asked to do things outside of your comfort zone. You will find yourself having to be humble. Having to own up to what you did wrong so you can move forward. I had to take a good look at who I was. God had a bigger purpose for me and I was going down the wrong path when I was younger. Once God comes in and says it is time to "Go", even if it means prison, know there is power in that purpose.

When the Judge let me go, I was vindicated in everything I had believed. I was told I would be released that day and I was. I had a fresh start. I had a clean slate. I had a real sense of Christianity, not just going to church, alive within me again.

I left prison to come to Atlanta with nothing. I had no money. I had no place of my own. God had instructed me to, again, to "Go" and again I listened. It was hard to listen. Food and survival almost hours from running out and becoming homeless. When I started to doubt my decision to listen to God, I was again amazed.

God said he would provide for me if I did as he said. When the walls started to close in on me, my instinct and my mind went right back to rationing out reasons to lie, cheat, and steal. I started to think of ways to scheme and scam money to eat and to live by. I had to remind myself of who was really in the driver's seat.

God wasn't about to let me fail. I said, "Lord, I am going to trust you." As soon as I spoke those words and handed my worry over to God, he started sending me everything I needed; money and help was coming out of nowhere. Everything worked out and I never had a reason to doubt this, although I was tempted to do so.

For those reading this right now, with the weight of the world so heavy upon you now, know that you only trust the word of God. The simple act of continued obedience to how God is driving you forward in life will uplift you and elevate your place- even when that "Go" means having to stay still and wait for the Judge to release you."

SHINING THROUGH THE STORM

A Word on Persistence

NOW THAT I'VE SHARED my story - and the stories of other women who stepped out on faith - along with many reference points of the Bible to help you understand what to do when God says "Go"; you can start to create the life you want!

There were times in my life that I was put on hold. God literally called me, I answered, and then there was mute silence. Imagine the frustration on my end. This is where perseverance and persistence have to be injected into your life and how you think and operate. You can't roll with the punches if you don't know how to keep yourself going. Expecting great things during times of crisis is a way to remain persistent in your obedience and belief in God.

Developing persistence is a master skill to success, but you can't do it without having strong faith in God. I know it is easier to relax and do nothing, or just live in your comfort zone, rather than face the uncertainty and discomfort of sailing through our goals or listening to and following the Holy Spirit. I've cut corners. It doesn't work. You have to be up for the challenge, too.

To develop persistence and eventually succeed, I have found that you must be positive and seek God in prayer at all time. Keep your thoughts focused on God and all things that produce a happy and peaceful life. God is not the author of confusion; God is a God of love and peace. Avoid negative thoughts and people, for these toxic things will ruin and distract your life.

If it seems that your life is at a standstill, just simply trust God and know that all things are working together for the good. When God seems distant and/or doesn't answer our prayers as quickly as we would like, the Bible teaches that we are to wait patiently and submit ourselves fully to God and trust his ways in all that we do. This is a direct act of faith. The Bible also tells us that all who have been "born again" have eternal security and will persevere, if we are persistent, because of our faith as Christians.

Years ago, when I started ThinkZILLA PR & Consulting Group, I found it challenging because I wasn't always the type of person that wanted to network and meet new people. I was experienced, but I was a new product and new face on the market in the marketing and PR Industry. I started to pray and ask God for guidance. I questioned, was this really what I should be doing? Is this what God have called me to do? Remember that your purpose never starts with you. Zig Ziglar says it best, "You can get everything in life you want, if you will just help enough other people get what they want."

It seemed I would never see my dream of helping others build their dreams come true. I was always trying to see the end from the beginning. That's not the way God works. You will never see the end from the beginning, but if you will have faith, everything else will work itself out. I remember sometimes I would just sit quietly and wait on God to tell me what to do next, and in every situation, that worked amazing. The amazing thing about God is that if you seek him, you will find him. I have experienced this first hand.

Do not allow the devil to plant seeds of discouragement in your mind. God is in control of everything, even our success. Often, we want things to happen fast, but remember we cannot force God to do things on our time. All we can do is sit patiently, follow his lead, be still when needed, and persistent the rest of the time. We must focus on trusting God always. Everything will happen in God's perfect timing.

Most people have a false perception of what success is. My definition of success is simple: "GOD is my CEO". There are no losses in the kingdom of heaven. Succeeding in life is about doing everything as though you are working for God. If you align 95% of your efforts to pleasing God, you will start to notice a huge change in your life.

Here are the true keys to success; always pray, be kind, be humble, forgive others, be loyal, trust god, and work hard at what you do. God's big plan for your life will require that you carry your own cross. It will never be easy, but keep on working at it. Look at the women and the stories shared in this book. There was doubt. There were tests. There were valid reasons to give up on their "Go" moments. We are all flawed, just like you, and we are all bonded by our ability to be persistent and consistent with our faith and obedience.

Major success seldom comes easily or without a great deal of effort. Often the only difference between those who succeed and those who don't is the ability to keep going long after the rest have dropped out. Life is like a marathon race. Either you have the stamina to complete the race, or you give up. The good news is that with God you can work on your personal and professional stamina, so when he does say "Go" you can not only run your race, but you can see it through to the end, too.

Some people want success so badly that they never look for an excuse or a way out. What keeps highly effective people going is their powerful level of desire, which can be sparked by their 'why'. Have you thought about your why in life? It could be your children or to help the less fortunate. What is your purpose? What is your why? Remember that your purpose will never start with *you*. I have heard so many stories of when God put a dream in a heart, a passion in the pit of the stomach, or spoke to the person directly, only to have everything result in repeated failures and dead ends. These life-teasers (as I like to call them) happen for a reason.

Persistent people have the inner energy and intensity to keep them motivated and going through tough times because of their relationship with God. Scripture tells us, 'If God be for you, who can be against you?' Persistent people are often dreamers and visionaries who see their lives as having a higher purpose than simply earning a living or making money. Most people do things because of the money, and that is the wrong motivator for anything in life.

If you are doing something just for the money, you will always get burned out. Don't let money be your motivator. The Bible tells us the God is a jealous God, and that we are sinning if we worship two Gods and money is God to some. Now this doesn't mean you can't be wealthy, it simply means seek God, and everything else will fall in place; you should be building from a heavenly system and not a worldly system.

If you walk with God, you will see such favors and grace enter your life. You will start to see things differently. You will start to experience peace. If you are experiencing a rough time, or are in the middle of facing serious life altering situations - know that God has his eye on you, and he will never put more on you than you can bear. Every challenge is an opportunity to become a better person. Every opposition you face should teach you something. There is significant treasure in troubles, be open to learning the lesson behind the trouble.

Many of us have been through moments where it seems like everything is at a stand still, even though you *know* you've been working hard. For me, that's one of the most discouraging feelings ever, and if you are not careful, you will fall into the devil's trap. Stand strong and have faith! God's plans are so much greater than ours, and often we can't see what God is doing, but if you have faith, you will see everything fall into place.

There will always be storms that cross your path. No one gets to breeze through life easily, but with God, you will not face these problems alone. Life can be draining, life can also be depressing; daily, we are faced with so many decisions. At times, it is difficult to stay motivated, and when it appears that no progress is being made and problems keep popping up, sometimes we want to throw in the towel. There are plenty of days that I just wanted to give up. It seemed the minute I started to pray, the angels would pick me up and I would have a burst of new energy.

When you deeply commit yourself, be obedient, and stay hopeful; you start to appreciate your relationship with God, you experience your heavy loads being lifted. I lean on God for everything; he will never run low of resources and patience. I have learned to make God the focal point of my life. The more you look to God, the more you experience a sense of newness, you become more refreshed, and your steps will always be firm, sure, and steady. Even though the world around you seems to be tumbling in a whirlwind of troubles, you will always find your balance in Christ.

Finally, you *must* pray for perseverance; there *will* be people in your life who have critical eyes. God's true people usually stand out from the crowd, and are often misunderstood or ridiculed because they can make those around them feel uncomfortable. Not everyone will be able to go where God is taking you.

Each person's purpose and mission is different, and some people are holding you back. Often, we are afraid to let go of old friends and habits, but to have something you've never had before; you must be willing to do something you've never done. A new life will require a new version of you. God will bring new friends and good, Godly people into your life. But first, you must make room by ridding yourself of everything and everyone that is holding you back.

GODLY BUSINESS BATTLES

A Word to the Wise

YOU CAN'T RUN A BUSINESS without God. In fact, you should not do anything without seeking God first! Psalm 37:23-24 (NIV) says, "The LORD makes firm the steps of the one who delights in him; though he may stumble, he will not fall, for the LORD upholds him with his hand."

You may be in a business now that makes tons of money, but you are reading this book for a reason. Maybe you are seeking to start a business, but are not sure how you will without the proper resources or money. Being in business requires determination, passion, and strength; all these things come from God. None of this is possible *without* God. You must be humble, rid yourself of pride, and always keep a positive mindset. Without His guidance, the ability to be tempted into bad decisions led by greed and ego will be too great and eventually destroy your personal life and business.

You can't 'fake it until you make it'! There is a saying in the Greek culture about asking for help or pleading ignorance. It goes "Don't cry wolf too often or people will doubt your sincerity." Why am I bringing this in my personal story of God's divine intervention? I want you to understand the power of testimony over not only your life, but also the life of someone else. And yes, I also want you to understand that you can't fake your way through life; God gives grace and wisdom to those who are humble.

It is never good to cry wolf. Some people cry wolf in the most untraditional sense. They say they are happy and lovely and that all is going well in their life, but deep down inside they aren't okay. No one can help you if they don't know what you are going though. I'm not saying go tell everyone your business; I'm simply saying, faking it will get you nowhere.

Unfortunately, people cry wolf all the time. We have all been guilty of this at one time or another. But let me write frankly about this now in an attempt to help save you from unnecessary challenges in the future. Each time you cry wolf, manipulate others, and or pretend to be something that you are not - you are doing damage to your own reputation. You are not fooling anyone but yourself. And most importantly, God sees and knows all.

Being fake harms the ability for people to help you, authenticity is so important. No one wants to deal with a fake person. It only delays your growth and it allows the devil to slide into your life. Again, pride. We want to think of ourselves as superheroes. We sometimes overcommit, or tell an untruth to back out of something, instead of being honest with our peers. These untruths or exaggerations cause us to be stressed and not blessed.

"Go" moments come when we are honest with others and ourselves. The Bible specifically talks about being truthful in our endeavors. Being truthful allows us to interact with others with grace and not greed or deception as motivators.

You cannot pass "Go" if you are not honest with yourself and with others about your plight in life and about who you are as a person. Once you are honest with yourself and with others, God can promote you. He can show mercy towards you. He can help you realize the path to his Kingdom.

My final piece of advice, and a big part of this shared story, is to encourage you to drop the pride. Stand still and listen for God. If he is silent, pray. And continue to pray. Don't lose faith or stop trusting if your prayers are not answered right away. Trust in God and remember that all things are working together for your good. Your success in life is dependent on your obedience to God.

We can't always time our "Go" moments, but you've picked up this book for a reason. I believe in divine intervention. When your "Go" moment arrives (and it will), regardless of how difficult the journey may be (or how much sense it doesn't make), show faith with persistence and follow what God puts in your heart.

MY STEPS FOR "GO" SUCCESSES WITH GOD

I N YOUR "GO" MOMENT, don't overlook being faced with temptation. Jesus himself had his own "Go" experience, starting with 40 days and nights of fasting, and that was exactly when the tempter came; afterwards, he started his ministry fully - as documented in the text we will consider.

I had my own "Go" experience too, but before my second chance at life. I discarded my consecration (I was supposed to stay away from anything business and remain in prayer like Jesus; he had been fasting for forty days and nights). I broke my consecration; I decided to take on the engagement, which led to the crash. If we don't learn to overcome temptation, I assure your life will be totally devastated.

God does not promise that we will never be tempted, but that when we are, He will provide a way of escape. As Christians, there are things we can do to avoid unnecessary temptation. Temptation can often be completely avoided by following these simple tips.

Pray: In the model prayer that Jesus gave to his disciples in Matthew 6, He taught them to ask God to lead them away from temptation (Matthew 6:13). A daily relationship with God in prayer is a first step to avoiding temptation.

Notes: I mentioned this in chapter 3; the power of prayer is your armor. You must use it daily, use it wisely, and you need to be honest about what you are, who you are, and whose child you are when praying. Don't pray for what you want, ask God to allow his Holy Spirit to teach you how to pray. I have shared ten personalized prayers at the end of this book that changed my life drastically and they will change yours, too. Consider what Jesus was doing before he encountered the tempter- he had been fasting for 40 days and nights (need I say, he was praying too).

Use the Word of God: There are many good verses that will help you overcome certain temptations. Memorizing Bible verses targeted to combat your areas of temptation will be a wonderful protection and defense. 2 Corinthians 10:4-5 talks about demolishing arguments and pretensions that try to get a stronghold in your life. You need to work on memorizing a list of Bible verses that will help you avoid temptation. You cannot rely on having a Bible in hand at the moment of temptation; these verses have to become second nature to you. Spend time with God's word daily. Make it a habit. By knowing the Bible will confront you in your reading tomorrow, can help you stay focused on God today.

Notes: if your disposition to God's word is to only learn memory verses, that's not the best way to approach studying God's word. 'You can *just* memorize Bible verses, but they will lack power unless you study your Bible, and learn to deeply and truly understand the Word of God.' But when you study God's word, knowing these verses becomes second nature to you; when temptation arises, you will know exactly what to say. Do you not see how Jesus replied to the devil each time? Even when the devil tried to twist scriptures in a bid to make Jesus fall into his trap, Jesus remained in faith and not temptation.

Understand Your Personal Weaknesses: Not everyone is tempted in the same way. What is a struggle for one person may not be the least bit tempting to another person. For example, one person may be tempted with smoking. For the next guy, smoking has never had a foothold on the person, and therefore is not at all tempting, but he may be tempted by something else, like alcohol.

James 1:14 says that we are drawn away by our own lusts. This indicates that each person has his or her own weaknesses to deal with. You need to understand your own weakness so you will know how to combat and avoid it.

Notes: If you don't have a weakness, you're likely not human or you have an impressive case of denial happening. Yes, we are children of God, but clothed in flesh. We all have weaknesses, we don't glory in them; but e need to understand them so we can apply the word of God.

Flee Temptation: God has promised to make a way to escape temptation. If you find the escape route then you can flee the temptation. Often, this escape route is to literally walk (or run) away. Temptation often comes when you find yourself in certain situations or places. When you recognize one of those situations, it is time to pack up your stuff and get out of there.

Notes: Don't allow the word temptation to confuse you. the definition of Temptation is a desire to do something, especially something wrong or unwise. There are often certain things that trigger temptation and those are the things we should avoid also. Never think you are strong enough to completely ignore the urge of being tempted, it's an everyday fight.

Create an Accountability Network: As Believers, we have direct access to God. There is no place in the Bible where we are taught that we must confess our sins to others to gain forgiveness from God. However, the Bible does teach that creating accountability with someone else can help you in your struggle against temptation (James 5:16).

You do not need to go into deep detail with your accountability partner about your struggles, but they do need to know how to pray for you. Find someone who is a mature Christian. Often your pastor or small groups at your church can fill this role, but it can also be a trustworthy friend. Tell them that you are struggling in a certain area. Look through the Bible together to find verses that will help you. Have your friend ask you occasionally how you were doing in this area; once a week is usually enough. Make a promise to your friend that you will not lie to them when asked about how you are doing.

Don't be discouraged: You should not become complacent about your sin. But you should also not allow it to defeat you. Sin is much more serious than eating too much dessert, but it allows me to make an analogy. If you are on a diet and eat an extra cookie, does it make sense to quit your diet and gorge on the rest of the bag? The truth is that one extra cookie is a minor thing compared to how many good choices you made the previous week. It sounds silly to quit a diet because of 100 extra calories. Yet, people do it all the time.

Realize that you probably will fall to temptation on occasion, but that is no reason to quit your Christian journey. Don't treat your sin as if it doesn't matter, but also realize that you have a choice in your future actions.

Notes: Don't *ever* be discouraged. Jesus' death was for you and it tells you sin has been defeated. That you are faced with temptation does not mean you have sinned, that you have sinned does not mean you have lost the battle. No! In fact, you should exercise Jesus' victory over sin.

Confess and Repent: When you fall into temptation, go to God and confess. He already knows about your sin. You are not telling Him anything that is a surprise. But for your own sake, you should humble yourself before God and confess your sin. The truth is, He has already forgiven you if you're a Christian. Going to Him in confession makes it easier for you to have clear communication with Him.

Notes: Jesus already defeated sin; therefore in God's heart, our sins are forgiven. However, this point helps you, not God; it helps your conscience, so you can move on. It's not like you have to inform God, he knows what you've done.

As believers, you should realize that you have the strength to withstand temptations. Realizing you have the power to overcome is the first step to not accepting defeat. No matter the addiction or weakness, the power of the cross is greater; redemption has afforded us great victory over sin. We only need to embrace this. The devil was never able to defeat Jesus, not even once-that means Jesus taking your place on the cross, now affords us the luxury to live his life as well; you also have the ability to overcome temptation and exercise victory.

"When Jesus died, he took sin down with him, but alive he brings God down to us. From now on, think of it this way: Sin speaks a dead language that means nothing to you; God speaks your mother tongue, and you hang on every word. You are dead to sin and alive to God. That's what Jesus did." (Romans 6:10-11)

"GO" TOWARDS YOUR PURPOSE

I HAVE ALWAYS HAD the entrepreneurial spirit and the ambition since I was a teenager; I always knew working for someone else would probably not work for me. In my early twenties, my first job ever was working with Google, then I worked in collections; and that was the end of working for someone. After that, I pursued my dreams and have failed quite a bit, but I never gave up. Today, I am thankful for the failures because I can help others avoid those pitfalls, failures, and mistakes. So again, God is using all of my failures and bad decisions in life to help others.

My whole life I have had to stop, "Go", and then start again. If you are experiencing or waiting on your "Go" moment, know that it may not be your only "Go" moment. Until we take our last breath in life, God is always molding and shaping us. You will be called to serve in so many ways throughout this life. I know I have.

For me, "Go" has always been an action word. I have leaned on God when I didn't trust Him and leaned on Him even further when I did. My life lesson with these moments has always been about trusting Him- even when the possibilities seemed unlikely or restraints seemed too much to bear.

God loves it when you trust and obey Him! God loves it when you rely on Him to take you through life's journey. He rewards faith, and the quicker you trust and obey; the sooner you'll reap the benefit of His blessing. During this past year, when I had to "Go", I have learned that the principle of "accelerated blessing"- as described in my Church- can only be possible when we are ready to receive the blessings.

When we value who we are and act in the spirit of the Lord, we can start to listen and see what God truly wants for us and from us in life. I know it is easy to become impatient and want God to do something for us right now, but we forget about God's purposes and God's timing. We don't understand why it's taking God so long to answer our prayers or we get frustrated when what we want is not what we end up with.

My "Go" journey has been about giving as much as it has been about receiving. I have worked so hard to uplift others. I wanted to include the personal trials and tribulations of the celebrated women mentioned in this book because we can all learn from their stories and give glory to God.

Divorce is never easy. Few divorces, as amicable as they can be, end with a happy "Go". I know three couples that divorced happily, and are still close. I don't know for all of them, but at least one couple did have separate "Go" moments during the process. I do realize that these couples are the exceptions to the rule. When I was going through my divorce, there were positive moments, but there were a lot of negative things I had to revisit. The "Go" was a bittersweet goodbye to that chapter of my life. It is a chapter worth revisiting now, it had lessons for me as far as my behavior and what I will and will not tolerate in a relationship going forward. That "Go" was painful with prayer, but I had to move forward.

Divorce doesn't have to be from a spouse. I think the most important thing I learned about my recent series of God saying "Go" is that the "Go" can be a way for you to divorce from a lesser version of yourself. It is a way to move up and help others do the same. You have to face some ugly truths and leave behind some immature notions, but - in the end - the divorce can be a good thing.

Discovering my purpose was easy. I knew how to spot my talents. I knew they shouldn't be muted. But for others, this purpose isn't always so crystal clear. I talk about finding your "Go" moment, as I had to do. The next question then is where do you start? What questions do you use to open up a conversation with God about if it is time for you to have a "Go" moment or not?

Think about where you are now. Do you have a good relationship with God? Do you have a right relationship with your spouse? A good relationship with your family? A good relationship with your church? How about a good relationship with people at your workplace? We all have work to do and God moves those who need the most growth and who will be responsible enough to honor Him after their growth.

I pretended for a long time that I was all right. I was done pretending. I am sure many of you can relate to me and my words. Are you preparing yourself to listen for God's "Go"? Before you answer, think about the question.

What are you doing to prepare yourself for a life-altering event? I know, before the crash, I was preparing to meet a client. I was back in my state of pride and disobedience. I was trying to take on the world by myself, only to come home at night and pray for God to take the wheel. I forgot that His timing was not my timing, and that my timing is not His timing.

You may be standing at the door to the Promised Land today, but for some reason you haven't entered. It may be fear, it may be something else, but God is calling you. You picked up this book for a reason. My story appealed to you in some way. The next question is going to be what have you learned from what we have shared? Will you answer and "Go" when God calls? Or will you ignore his call, get into your car, and head out for a drink?

I wake up every day and I ask Jesus to allow me to remain in the prayer of faith throughout the day. I ask him to not let the evil one get a hold of me and not to allow myself to fall into the pitfalls of temptation, such as greed, ego, pride, doubt, and frustration. Why do I do this? Because my "Go" moment was the catalyst of my journey with Christ, not the destination.

To your "Go" moment… may you walk with the Peace of God knowing that He will provide all that you need.

TEN PRAYERS FOR REAL LIFE

I have written so much about me, my life, my story, and how God showed me when it was time to "Go". With all the direction I had, and the lessons I learned, I realized no one ever provided me with a template to prayer or how to pray. The following ten prayer formats to help you get started on your journey with God are my gift to you. These are your pre-"Go" prayers. Feel free to customize them however you wish, and share them with others along your path in life, too.

Velma's Prayer for Happiness:

Dear God, I come to you in prayer today, thanking you for everything that you've done for me and asking for happiness in my life. I know that true happiness comes from only you and the kingdom of heaven. Please direct my path each moment of this day.

Make me truly happy, put joy and peace on every path I take. May all my endeavors be met with happiness, may all my dealings be met with joy. Father, as I subscribe to my "Go" moment, may all the good things that come with happiness surround me. I have decided to give myself to you, I have decided to put all my trust in you, I have decided to "Go" where you want me to go, to do the things you want me to do, and I know that with obedience comes true happiness.

Lord, teach me to not seek happiness in the wrong places, may your kind and gentle hand continue to lead me on the path of true happiness and joy. May the happiness you pour into my life grant me understanding, wisdom, and knowledge above all things. May my happiness cause me to have love for others, may my happiness put unlimited joy in my heart. Guide me, Lord, into

true happiness, and your praise will never depart from my lips, neither will I stop telling others how great you are. You are my rock, and I thank you for loving me.

In Jesus' name, Amen.

Velma's Prayer for Prosperity

Dear Heavenly Father, I come to you in prayer today, thanking you for everything that I have and everything that I don't have. I pray that you will lead me to prosperity and all things good, because I know that every good and perfect gift comes from you. Lord, I ask today that you prosper my business, and everything that I lay my hands upon. Bless all my deals and teach me to align everything that I do with the purpose that you have for my life. May all I do yield returns beyond my expectations.

Lord, I ask that you prosper anything that my heart set out to do. Train me today to be great, guide my heart into the right ventures. Teach me to be able to discern between what's right and what's wrong. Be the rock of my business, Father. Be my protector against all who would take me for granted. Shield and protect me from anything that would cause me to fail. Bless me Father and make me prosperous, just like you. I will forever love you, praise you, and seek your holy name.

I pray that everything I touch will multiply; I pray that my blessings will cause me to be a blessing to many others across the world.

In Jesus' name I pray, Amen.

Velma's Pray of Faith

Dear God, my rock and my salvation. Your word teaches us to have faith in you and to walk by faith and not by sight. I come to you today because in faith I accepted my "Go" moment and have chosen to follow you.

I pray for strength through all my struggles and challenges this day. It is not easy Lord, but with hope and faith, I desire to walk closely with you, standing on your promises. I pray that you grant me the knowledge to know you, your power, and the extent of your love for me.

My God and My Lord, I look at the men of the Old Testament and I pray to earnestly have faith as strong as theirs.

Grant me faith like Abraham, when he obeyed you and left his descendants. Grant me faith like Noah, when he built the ark without question. Grant me faith like Joshua and Caleb, when they brought a positive report from Canaan, against what their eyes had seen. Grant me faith like David, when he faced the giant, Goliath. Grant me faith like all our spiritual leaders, who believe in you and serve you.

Father, may my faith in you only get stronger with each new day, may my desire to obey you continue to grow. I pray that I will live in prosperity, joy, peace, and an overflow of abundance all my life.

In Jesus' name I pray, Amen.

Velma's Prayer for Discernment

Dear Lord, I pray for discernment, so I may serve you well. I pray for discernment, so that I may know your will. I pray for discernment, so that I may know your voice, just like the sheep knows the voice of its shepherd.

Grant me discernment and knowledge so that I may know your will and meditate on the wonderful things you have done for me. David, your servant, knew discernment and with this, he served you well and conquered all his enemies. Father, I pray for your discernment, in every decision and move I make.

Teach me to have discernment in all my relationships, my investments, and businesses.

Teach me to know discernment, even amongst those who pretend to like me, but really have plans to harm me. As an ambassador for you, Lord, teach me your ways. Forgive me for all my sins. I am far from perfect, but I desire to change, and become more like you. Allow me to lean, not on my own understanding, but on you My Lord.

In Jesus' name I pray, Amen.

Velma's Wisdom Prayer

Dear Lord, above all else I seek wisdom. I pray for the wisdom that comes from you, not the wisdom of this world. You said in your word that anyone that seeks wisdom would surely find it. Father, today I pray and yearn for wisdom. Teach me wisdom Lord, because I am lost without you.

I have made the wrong decisions in my past, and sometimes I still make the wrong decisions. I know that, without wisdom, I will be a complete failure. Lord have mercy on me, renew my mind and my heart. Clean my heart and make it pure, so that everything that comes out of my mouth will uplift others.

May my obedience come with an overflowing of wisdom from you. May my heart meditate in the wisdom of your power, may my mouth only speak wise words of understanding.

May all my decisions be well thought out decisions, inspired by your word and will for me.

Father, you gave Solomon, your servant, wisdom and with his wisdom he did right before you and laid a foundation that we all still learn from to this day.

Like Solomon, grant me wisdom and foresight, so that all I do today will be remembered thousands of years from now. I pray that people of coming generations may also learn and be guided by the works you will do through me in this season of my life. Bless me Lord with your wisdom.

In the name of Jesus I pray, Amen.

Velma's Prayer for Increase

I come to you in prayer Lord Jesus, because you are my father, my lord, and my rock. Because I have faith, I believe that everything I ask for will be granted because of my obedience. Today, I decree that all I do will flourish.

I decree an increase in every area of my life. Even though right now I am struggling financially I believe that a breakthrough will happen in your timing. Until then, Lord give me strength to keep on pushing.

Father, I pray that you will increase me and enlarge my territory with every new day. Father, I pray that my all of my increase will be blessed and no obstacle will pull me back. I will climb to the top, and I will reach the peak of all my desires and aspirations. I pray this day, that your grace and divine power will be my guide and protector as I walk the path of my "Go" moment. Nothing will hinder my definite increase, nothing will slow it down, and nothing will steal from it. My rise to the top will be continuous and unstoppable.

I commit all my dealings into your hands, Dear Father, take them as your own, and take me as your own, so that nothing will hinder your will in my life.

In the name of Jesus I pray, Amen.

◆

Velma's Forgiveness Prayer

Dear Lord, have mercy on me. Please forgive me for all my sins. I repent and ask for a fresh start and a new beginning. I pray that I will no longer be alive to sin, but that you will show me the way to a heavenly lifestyle.

I have gone astray at times, and have been disobedient to your commandments, I acknowledge my wrongs today, and I lay them at your feet because I know you can save me from my sins and grant me the joy that comes with salvation. Save me from my sins today, Father, because of your love for us. Forgive my wrongs, Lord, and teach me how to get back on track and not be distracted by the devil's schemes and games. Put me in the full armor of God, so that I can stand up and be strong.

Have mercy on me, Lord, and forgive my sins. Today Father, I open my heart before you and I let go of any grudges or anger that surrounds my inner being. I let go of my attachment to sin and all the things that make me sin against you. As you wash away my sins and make me clean, I renew my commitment to my "Go" moment and I rededicate myself to serving you and doing your will.

Thank you father, because I know I am a new me and all my sins are forgiven.

In the name of Jesus, Amen.

Velma's Overcoming Temptation Prayer

Dear Lord, I come to you in prayer today because I know you are the author and finisher of our faith. I know you are my Lord and protector against all the paths of the devil. As I embrace my "Go" moment, I know the devil is not happy and will throw all sorts of temptation in my face.

I know that you are with me every step of the way. I pray, Lord, that you grant me the strength, foresight, wisdom, and understanding to overcome all the temptation of the enemy.

I pray, Lord, that you will make things plain and clear. And even when the enemy distracts me, I will quickly whisper your name so that you will bring me back along the right path.

I pray, Lord, that the Holy Spirit will guide my actions, and when evil looks at me, I will be strong enough to resist temptations. I pray to be victorious over all temptations and distractions that come my way.

In Jesus' name I pray, Amen.

Velma's Courage Prayer

Dear Lord, I come to you in prayer today because I am fearful and sometimes discouraged. I know that fear is a trick of the devil. I fear failure; I sometimes fear what people may say or think about me. I fear stepping out on faith because I don't know what the results will be.

Lord, you are my refuge and my protector. You are my rock; you will fight all my battles.

I pray for divine courage through all my fears, challenges, and obstacles. I ask for courage so that I may be able to stand strong, no matter how embarrassing it seems. I ask for courage today Lord, so that I may be able to proclaim your name and praises, no matter what people say.

Father God, grant me the courage I need to serve you with all my heart and soul.

Grant me the courage to be a successful ambassador of your will. Grant me the courage to overcome every seed of fear, doubt, and disbelief.

In the name of Jesus, I pray, Amen.

Velma's Relationship Prayer

Dear Lord, your word says, "Love conquers all", and I know that I cannot serve you if I do not have love in my heart. I come to you today in prayer, asking that you will put love in my heart. Put your love in my heart, Father, so that I will learn to be patient and prayerful by everything that I do.

Put your love in my heart, so that I will be kind. Put your love in my heart and wipe away every sign of pride, guilt, or arrogance. Put your love in my heart, and make me selfless and humble. Put your love in my heart, so that I won't be easily angered, and I won't hold grudges against others.

Put your love in my heart, so that I will always love the truth and hate what is evil.

Put your love so that I will always trust you, have faith in you, and always put my hopes in you.

Father, may your love in my life never fail, no matter the kind of hatred or wickedness I encounter. May your love in my life continue to grow stronger with each new day, teaching me to love my enemies and those who spitefully use me.

In the name of Jesus I pray, Amen.

GOD'S PROMISE AND THE REWARD OF THE DESTINATION

———✳———

THIS ISN'T THE END of my journey, in fact it is the beginning; and it is *your beginning*. Like my story, it doesn't matter where you have been in life or where you are now, things can change with the mighty power of God. Your "Go" moment is owed to you by faith, not by necessity. My car was totaled. I could have been dead. I had faith. While it looked like a punishment, God was setting me up to reap the rewards of my faith. What in your life looks like a battle or a punishment that could really be a blessing in disguise? Is your view on life negative or Godly? The view of surviving my car accident is pleasant, because it has a Godly association.

If you've learned anything from my story, and the lessons noted within the pages of this book, your outlook defines your life. Are you looking at challenges as punishments? Or are you looking at problems as victories to come? God may set you up for a lesson, but it is always for your betterment. It is so you can handle your next success and elevate others, too. Your attitude should always be one of gratitude as God is the creator of all things and every situation. He will not let you fail.

One of the strongest passages in the Bible comes from Psalms 50:15, which reads;

"And call upon me in the day of trouble: I will deliver thee, and thou shalt glorify me." God creates opportunities for those who are faithful; and sometimes not so gentle reminders (like my accident), that He is calling for us to walk a path in His honor during our life here on Earth.

Like me, your "Go" moment may be painful at first. It may seem like more of a lesson than a blessing. My "Go" moment was both spiritually and physically painful. Living the life I led, I could have perceived the car wreck to be a punishment of God for being disobedient and not listening to the Spirit regarding working on that particular day. The pain of the accident was the rebirth of me. It was a literal and spiritual crash into my own personal victory!

What I encourage you to remember every day when you wake up is that you can't set yourself up for rewards without calling out to God during times of trouble. You may not agree with the way he delivers answers to your prayers, but he always delivers! Also remember that God will not be able to answer your prayers if you don't speak to God and have a relationship with him, I mean a real relationship. While I thought my vision in life was to live amongst the entertainment sector with my marketing and public relations talents, my "Go" moment and victory have been the new dreams and visions put into my spirit. I've pivoted my professional plans and improved my personal life. Now, instead of using my gifts on whatever I want to use them on, I really serve God. My company now specializes in helping churches and Christian based businesses grow by bridging the gap between the secular landscapes. We are the Christian marketing experts. All I can say is BUT GOD! There is purpose to my life and, outside of simply making a living I am walking in my Purpose.

Yes, from Houston to Atlanta, with a dream in my heart and a hunger for God, I can honestly say my current journey isn't invested in material things, but I've invested in personal development and spiritual growth and now I completely rely upon my higher power, God, and the work He puts in my path helps to not just to survive but to thrive, all while helping to spread the message of God.

I've been able to acquire more true friendships, understand healthy relationships and boundaries, and I am used as a vessel of service for churches and entrepreneurs that need a market-centric branding specialist who has walked the walk. My "Go" moment had purpose and I am now happier than I have ever been. It took some pain to get to true peace and real happiness.

You've picked up this book for a reason. Maybe you're not ready to join the "Go" community on my website, but there is a sense of something greater buried in you, NEVER FORGET THAT! God had to wake me up, too. I had to learn lessons and earn every single victory within my life after the accident. No, it hasn't been easy, but it has been amazingly rewarding and worth every single faith-based step!

There are moments in life when you realize the struggle is real. Maybe it is at these times that God is choosing the right to remain silent in our life. Don't get frustrated. Do not revert to old habits, or even worse, new vices. Don't give in to the heaviness that may grow, like mold, under your skin; taunting you to give up. Instead, stay in faith. Accept the silence you may be experience and understand that He will speak your "Go" moment when it is truly your time to reap rewards and arrive at your life's destination. Even if your growing pains feel like punishments, stay in the right attitude, and step out in faith, believing there is a reason for the season. At the right time, God will show you the why behind whatever it is you are going through right now.

During the storms, the heavy silence, and even when God is raining down rewards, I've learned that it is our duty to be thankful and to remain with a pure heart at all times and in every situation. My journey has been tough, but I've met the love of my life as a result. I'm ready to address some childhood issues. I'm willing to share who I am, insecurities and all, with like-minded people who also accept that God is complete control of not only their lives, but their businesses, too.

Change is hard; growth even harder. Life isn't for sissies. The presence of God will not provide an all-encompassing shade for you. People give up on God because they get it wrong when it comes to having faith. Faith is understanding and relying upon what you can't see or don't understand. When my Lexus was destroyed, I didn't understand it. Considering the gravity of the situation, I knew I was left on this Earth for a reason. Every day I wake up to happy children, a valid and honorable purpose in commerce, dreams to expand opportunities for others using my talents in real estate, and knowing that I am finally happy. I wake up with my faith and I pray several times throughout the day. I own my past mistakes and I proudly share them. I know my testimony is a victorious confirmation for someone else seeking a change in their life. I speak loudly and proudly about who I am, where I have been, and how my obedience to God took me to places I didn't understand, but to places that have all led me to a new life, a new love, and a reason to sing His name in praise every single day!

Your reward, your destiny - it is all within reach, regardless of the number of detours that it may take for you to reach it. The realization that we are not in complete control of our lives can be like touching a high-voltage fence. We don't want to do it, but remember that don't want to and can't are two different concepts. You can open yourself up to obtaining your goals and living a quality life. There will be discomfort and people who will badger or tempt you, but your faith during any silent pause or crashing storm in your life is all you need to keep you headed for success on your journey.

The mistakes I made in my personal life and with my business are all lessons, but they are also the foundational stepping-stones of my victories. These challenges are not roadblocks or punishments from God, they are opportunities to pass "Go", so you will know and appreciate when you reach your God intended destination.

You have a choice right now. You can say you've read this book and continue on with your life as normal. You can also choose to stand in faith and listen for when God calls you to "Go". God has granted us free will. Embracing the "Go" from God is what will define who you are, how you are, and if you will live an ordinary life or an extraordinary one. With prayers of faith knowing that you're ready to "Go" from inspired to an ambassador of God's miraculous hand in your life, I send blessings onto you. - Velma Trayham